# ADOPTION
## A Journey of Faith
Julie L. Potter

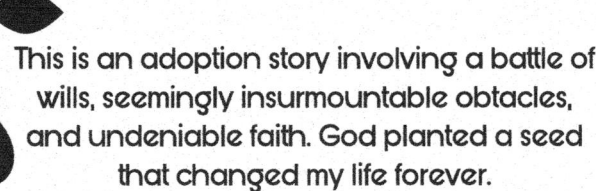

This is an adoption story involving a battle of wills, seemingly insurmountable obtacles, and undeniable faith. God planted a seed that changed my life forever.

First and foremost, I give all credit to God
who led me on this journey.

Secondly, to all the young women who have experienced an
unwanted pregnancy, making the difficult, emotional decision to
carry their baby to full term, only to give them up for adoption.
Thank you.

Finally, to my son, Cody, who inspired me.

# Table of Contents

Introduction .................................................. 1

Chapter 1 – God Speaks .......................................... 9

Chapter 2 – Our Happy Family ................................... 13

Chapter 3 – "20/20" ........................................... 17

Chapter 4 – That Question ..................................... 25

Chapter 5 – Who Am I? A Look Back ............................. 29

Chapter 6 – Seeking Direction ................................. 35

Chapter 7 – Dillon International ............................... 45

Chapter 8 – Family Meeting .................................... 53

Chapter 9 – The Process ....................................... 59

Chapter 10 – Remodeling ....................................... 67

Chapter 11 – Final Preparations ............................... 73

Chapter 12 – Destination: Ukraine ............................. 77

Chapter 13 – Kiev to Kharkiv by Train ......................... 91

Chapter 14 – Arrival: Kharkiv ................................ 101

Chapter 15 – The Orphanage ................................... 107

Chapter 16 – Let's Take a Tour ............................... 117

Chapter 17 – Charlie's Sick .................................. 127

Chapter 18 – Paperwork and Ice Cream ......................... 133

Chapter 19 – It's Official! .................................. 139

Chapter 20 – Final Days in Kiev .............................. 145

Chapter 21 – Warsaw, Poland .................................. 153

Chapter 22 – Let's Go Home ................................... 159

Chapter 23 – Just Give It Some Time .......................... 165

Confirmations ................................................ 185

Conclusion ................................................... 193

# Introduction

God has a plan. It's a perfect plan. However, He depends on imperfect humans to carry out His plan. How do we imperfect humans know what we're supposed to do in this life? How do we fit into His plan? How do we find out? The best answer I can offer to those questions is: read the Bible! It is His instruction manual. Then, engage with others who can offer spiritual guidance and wisdom. Find a local body of believers; a church where the Bible is exposited. Read books authored by men and women who have studied the ways of God and can lend their wealth of knowledge and spiritual insight. Finally, ask God by praying for His direction.

I am an imperfect human who listened to God's voice but struggled to understand exactly what He was asking me to do and even after I acknowledged what He was telling me, I had a hard time complying. Here are just a few examples of other imperfect humans God used to achieve His plan.

## Moses

In the second book of the Bible (Exodus), God gives a directive to Moses. Beginning at Exodus 3 (NIV), God is speaking to Moses;

(v.10) "So now, go. I am sending you to Pharaoh to bring my people the Israelites out of Egypt."

(v.11) But Moses said to God, "Who am I that I should go to Pharaoh and bring the Israelites out of Egypt?"

(v.12) And God said, "I will be with you...."

(v.13) Moses said to God, "Suppose I go to the Israelites and say to them, 'The God of your fathers has sent me to you,' and they ask me, 'What is his name?' Then what shall I tell them?"

God continues the exchange with Moses, providing detailed instructions. In Exodus 4, Moses still questions God;

(Ex 4:1) "What if they do not believe me or listen to me and say, 'The Lord did not appear to you'?"

God then gives Moses several miraculous signs to use to convince the Israelites, at which Moses again tries to reason with God.

(v.10) Moses said to the Lord, "Pardon your servant, Lord. I have never been eloquent, neither in the past nor since you have spoken to your servant. I am slow of speech and tongue."

(v.11) The Lord said to him, "....Now go; I will help you speak and will teach you what to say."

(v.12) But Moses said, "Pardon your servant, Lord. Please send someone else."

## Jonah

In the first chapter of the book of Jonah, God directs Jonah, son of Amittai: (v.2) "Go to the great city of Nineveh and preach against it, because its wickedness has come up before me."

(v.3) But Jonah ran away from the Lord....he found a ship still at port, ready to set sail....went aboard and sailed for Tarshish to flee from the Lord.

Much trouble ensued as Jonah tried to resist God's instruction. A great storm threatened to destroy the ship. The men onboard knew a powerful god must have a reason; surely someone on the ship was to blame for their peril. But who and why? Each man was questioned. Jonah told the men on the ship that he was running away from the Lord! The decision was made to throw him into the raging sea in order to save the ship.

After being tossed overboard, Jonah spent three days inside the belly of a large fish and finally cried out to God, asking for help. God answered Jonah's plea and saved him from certain death. Jonah finally submitted to God, but later argued with Him about the entire assignment. *Huh??* (Read the book of Jonah)

## Gideon

The account of Gideon is similar to that of Moses. In Judges 6, the Israelites have been oppressed once again by another group; the Midianites. Why? Because the Israelites have disobeyed God.

(Judges 6 v.1) The Israelites did evil in the eyes of the Lord, and for seven years he gave them into the hands of the Midianites.

When they are nearly without hope, starving in the desert, they cry out to God, asking for His help. God sends an angel.

(Judges 6 v.12) When the angel of the Lord appeared to Gideon, he said, "The Lord is with you, mighty warrior."

(v.13) "Pardon me, my lord," Gideon replied, "but if the Lord is with us, why has all this happened to us?...."

(v.14) The Lord turned to him and said, "Go in the strength you have and save Israel out of Midian's hand. Am I not sending you?"

(v.15) "Pardon me, my Lord," Gideon replied, "but how can I save Israel? My clan is the weakest in Manasseh, and I am the least in my family."

(v.16) The Lord answered, "I will be with you, and you will strike down all the Midianites, leaving none alive."

(v.17) Gideon replied, "If now I have found favor in your eyes, give me a sign that it is really you talking to me...."

Gideon becomes convinced by the signs the angel provides and follows the angel's instructions, but only out of fear. He completes a small task, but now God wants him to save Israel! That's a bit much.

(v.36) Gideon said to God, "If you will save Israel by my hand as you have promised—(v.37) look, I will place a wool fleece on the threshing floor. If there is dew only on the fleece and all the ground is dry, then I will know that you will save Israel by my hand, as you said." (v.38) And that is what happened. Gideon rose early the next day; he squeezed the fleece and wrung out the dew—a bowlful of water.

(v.39) Then Gideon said to God, "Do not be angry with me. Let me make just one more request. Allow me one more test with the fleece, but this time make the fleece dry and let the ground be covered with dew." (v.40) That night God did so. Only the fleece was dry; all the ground was covered with dew.

• • •

There are many more accounts throughout the Bible where men and women were given a directive from God, yet they had doubts, fears and questions. They were often confused and unsure, wanting more clarification. After all, they were imperfect humans. Can we blame them for not having enough faith to step out blindly into the unknown? I can't. Nor can I definitively say whether it's a good or bad idea to "put out a fleece" as Gideon did. I do believe we all need more faith. Can anyone ever have enough faith? God will clarify and confirm to us in however or whatever way He chooses. He tells us to do something; we know deep in our heart that it's Him, but we often run and hide. Why? We just don't have enough faith.

God gave me a directive in 1999 that would change my life forever. I didn't know anything about adoption. Neither my husband nor I had ever even considered adopting a child. I had no clue how to begin, where to go, or who to talk to. I didn't want to believe what God was telling me. I felt like Moses and Jonah and even Gideon. Did I "put out a fleece?" Yes. Did I have questions, doubts and fears? Yes. Did I need more faith? Yes! Did I run and hide? I sure tried!

Invariably, when someone asks about my children, I tell them about my three biological children, explaining that my fourth, youngest daughter, is adopted from Ukraine. I watch as their eyes widen and eyebrows go up and wait for the typical response,

"Really? How did that happen?" My answer is, "God did it. It's a long story." It rarely ends there. They still want to hear more.

I cannot tell you how many times I have thought about the young teenage mother who gave birth to a little girl in Ukraine in 1997, then gave her up for adoption. I think about what she must have gone through. I wonder what she felt after the decision was made to carry the baby to full term. Was she scared? Was she heartbroken? Was it the most difficult time in her life? How did she do it? Does she still think about that baby she gave birth to? Does she wonder what happened to her…where she is, how her life has turned out? *Of course she does!*

As I ponder all of this today, it occurs to me there are many other young women out there who have gone through the same thing. They chose to give their baby a chance at life rather than the alternative—an abortion. Choosing to save a life by carrying to full term, giving birth only to give their newborn away, must be one of the most difficult, heart-wrenching decisions a young woman finding herself in this situation will ever make.

Never in a million years did I think I'd adopt a child. It certainly was not part of *my* plan. I was perfectly content with my life and my family. Then God planted a seed. I doubted. I questioned. I pushed back. But, I was curious. I opened my mind and heart to God. I allowed Him to use me for His purpose. He only asked that I trust Him and let the seed grow.

As I look back now, I am able to see exactly how God accomplished His goal through me. I will share with you the unexplainable ways God confirmed, not only the adoption, but also the writing of this book. I don't know how God wants to use my work. I just know He does. This book is not about life or abortion choices. It is really not even about adoption. I am not advocating anything. I'm simply doing what God asked me to do—tell my story. The outcome is completely in His hands. He is in control—not me. Perhaps by sharing what happened to me, it will inspire you to grow your faith. And *that* is really what this book is about.

This story is true. I have chosen not to use real names of some of the professionals involved in order to provide anonymity. The dates and places are real. This is my adoption story involving a battle of wills, seemingly insurmountable obstacles, and undeniable faith. God had given me a clear directive so ultimately I answered, "Ok, Lord. Show me the way."

# CHAPTER 1

# God Speaks

## December, 2008

Every month, fifteen or so married couples from the church I belonged to would come together for potluck dinner and fellowship at our Sunday school teacher's home. We called our monthly get-together, "Sweethearts in Christ." My husband and I always enjoyed the food, fun, and fellowship. We especially liked the December gathering because everyone participated in a Christmas gift exchange. Each couple brought a gift and festive foods to share with each other. For a few hours, we ate, played games, shared stories, and prayed for each other. Charlie and I looked forward to "Sweethearts" each month.

As soon as everyone had arrived, our teacher prayed for the food and each of us lined up outside the kitchen, waiting to fill our plates. Charlie and I carried our plates into the den where extra chairs and tray tables were set up around the perimeter of the room and found a comfy place to sit and eat. I noticed a book on the end table next to me, lying alongside some Christmas decorations. The title grabbed my attention: *90 Minutes in Heaven* (Piper & Murphey, 2004). Curious, I set my plate of food on the edge of the end table and picked up the book, flipping it over to read the synopsis on the back cover. As I began to read, our Sunday school teacher's wife, Ruth Ann, came in with her plate and sat on the sofa next to me.

"Oh, I forgot I left that book here. I was trying to find it," she explained.

"Looks like a good book," I replied.

"I'm enjoying it," she said. "I recently bought it at an airport gift shop while I was waiting for my flight. A friend recommended it to me."

I looked at the cover again, mentally tucking it away in my mind, thinking I might pick up a copy when I finished the book I was currently reading.

A few weeks later, while out shopping for groceries and miscellaneous household items at our neighborhood Walmart, I passed by a book display at the end of one of the shopping aisles. As I glanced toward the shelf, I noticed the book I saw at "Sweethearts": *90 Minutes in Heaven. Oh yes, that's the book I wanted to read.* Pleased, I picked up a copy and placed it in the cart.

That same evening, I began to read Don Piper's amazing account of having actually died in a tragic car accident, his subsequent visit to heaven, and miraculous return to life. The description he gave of his 90 minutes spent in heaven was glorious. He then went on to describe the unimaginable pain he endured as he recovered from his multitude of injuries. I was enthralled.

One night, about halfway into the book, I found myself reading along when these words seemed to infiltrate the lines on the page: *"I want **you** to tell **your** story."* What? I looked up from the page, paused, looked back down and again an unspoken voice impressed on me, *"I want you to tell your story."* The words weren't there, but they was shouting out at me!

What just happened? I had never experienced anything like this before. I literally sat there in silence, frozen, not understanding what had just taken place. Clearly something just happened; God was speaking to me. I know how to pray and I know when God is working on me, usually by revealing my shortcomings or convicting me of my sins, but I've never had an experience quite like this.

Was He really speaking to me? Tell *my* story? What? About the adoption?

*"Yes."*

## CHAPTER 2

# Our Happy Family

I met Charlie in December, 1989. He asked me to marry him three days after we met! I thought he was crazy. Who is this tall, bearded red head? *Marry you? We just met!* It wasn't long, though, before his strong-willed Irish heart had won me over. He wasn't always the best at expressing his emotions, but his actions spoke volumes. Charlie did so much for others without being asked and there wasn't anything he wouldn't do for me. He continued asking me to marry him, relentlessly, until I finally gave in and said, "Yes." Seven months later, in August, 1990, we married.

We both loved our work. I knew I was going to be an artist by the time I was five years old. All I ever wanted to do was art and eventually made it my career. At the time, I was the graphics department manager in a large printing company located just a few miles from our comfortable three bedroom home in Broken Arrow, Oklahoma (just outside Tulsa). Charlie was a self-employed handyman. He performed many types of construction, remodeling and repairs on homes and small businesses in the area. Basically, he did just about anything and everything and if he didn't know how to do something, he'd figure it out. Both of us were experts in our respective fields.

My job was challenging and rewarding. Tackling several responsibilities at the same time kept me motivated and determined. The company I worked for printed millions of store marking labels that were distributed all throughout the country. I had my hands on nearly every link in the production chain, from talking directly with the customers who placed the orders, then creating the artwork and press schedules, to coordinating with the shipping department. I made sure the finished product moved out the door on time. I held myself to the highest of standards and thoroughly enjoyed being the manager of the Graphics Department.

Charlie loved serving his elderly clients. He said, "I want to help the widows because contractors are always taking advantage of them and it's just not right." He treasured the relationships he built with several widows, as well as widowers, around town. They would say to me, "I don't know what I'd do without Charlie." Whatever and whenever their need, he never hesitated to help them, often not charging them anything for his services. Once, one of the elderly widows called him in the middle of the night to ask if he would please come check her garage door. She wasn't sure if it was locked and was afraid someone might break in. He went. I knew he would. That's who he was. He had a giving heart and was the hardest working, most dedicated man I had ever known.

A year into our marriage, we were blessed with a son. If it had been a girl, I already had the name, Shelby, picked out.

Charlie chose the boy's name, Cody. Our son soon became the greatest joy in his dad's life. Charlie began taking Cody with him on jobs when he was only two years old! I worried about him being so young, traveling in a pickup truck to all those construction sites full of dangerous tools and machines, but would soon discover how much Cody loved going to work with his dad. I also found out the widows really enjoyed having Cody around so they could spoil him. Regardless of their motives, Cody and Charlie were definitely a hit with the elderly ladies.

When Cody turned four, Charlie and I realized he was exceptionally bright. He was able to figure change at the counter when Charlie paid for lunch at a fast food restaurant or bought supplies at a hardware store. One day, after I'd come home from work, Charlie came in with Cody and excitedly said to me, "Watch this. Our son can tell you how much money I put out here on the table." Charlie spread several denominations of bills and coins on the tabletop. I watched as Cody looked over the bills and coins, then proceeded to put them in the correct sequence and verbalize his addition, coming up with the right total!

"Wow! That's amazing!" I stated. "I don't think this is normal."

We decided to have our bright, blue-eyed, little "Einstein" evaluated through an "Exceptional Child Program" offered at a nearby university. When the testing was completed, the evaluators remarked at how well Cody performed and how at-ease he was with them, conversing in a confident, "adult-like" manner. His I.Q. rating was 138! I remarked, "He must have received the best genes from both his parents!" Charlie beamed with pride. *Yah, me too.*

The evaluators recommended we place Cody in a private school where he could excel, but we couldn't afford that. They suggested we apply for a scholarship, however, we really wanted him to grow up with his peers from our community. We lived in a great school district, so we ultimately made the decision to send him to public school. Cody became an avid reader and math was a breeze for him. He loved his teachers and they loved him. His second grade teacher called him her "little professor". Charlie and I were very proud parents.

Fast forward to 1999. Cody is now eight years old; a little Opie Taylor (very inquisitive) and a spitting image of his dad at that age. My older two children were grown and out of the house by then, each beginning their own adult lives. Charlie, Cody and I were content, just the three of us, living in our modest three bedroom home. We were involved in our local church. Our jobs were going well. Bills were getting paid. Everyone was healthy. Life in our little corner of the world was good. What more could we ask for? Yet, in early January, 1999, our happy little corner of the world was about to spiral into the unknown.

## CHAPTER 3

# "20/20"

## January, 1999

Friday, the end of a stressful work week, had finally arrived. I was tired and looking forward to the weekend. I arrived home around 6 p.m. and hauled in a load of paperwork I'd brought from the office, dumped it on the kitchen counter and hung my jacket on the coat tree in the entry. "Hey, I'm home!" I called out as I walked back to the kitchen, pondering what I could throw together for dinner.

I would often bring all the printing press schedules home in the evening so I could review them and add additional work as needed. Not only did I manage the Graphics Department, I was also responsible for having jobs ready to run on the presses for the next several days and weeks. One big rule in our twenty-four hour, seven day a week business, was to make sure those presses were never idle. I didn't want to do any work that evening, but I'd become accustomed to it and weekends were no exception.

After eating dinner together, my husband and son left the table and moved the short distance from the dining room to the living room to watch television. I finished clearing the dinner table, put away the leftovers, cleaned up, picked up my paperwork and spread it out on the kitchen table to review. There were copies of current schedules and miscellaneous reports to go through. I planned to sit there and focus on the weekly press schedules with Charlie and Cody close enough, I could still talk with them while I worked.

It was eight o'clock and *20/20* had just started on the television. I loved that program! I had forgotten it would be on that night. I enjoyed learning about current events and watching some of the hourly news shows that share information about what's happening in the world. *20/20* was one of my favorites.

I knew I had a lot of work to do, but I figured I could listen and work at the same time, right? *Right!* But wait! My son and husband didn't usually watch *20/20*. I was surprised they were actually going to watch it. I assumed they would get bored, start surfing channels soon and change to sports. I was wrong.

The topic of the show was, "Russian Orphanages." I listened as the investigative journalists began to describe the conditions of life inside orphanages in Russia. They stated, "All of the coverage we were about to see was done undercover." The workers and children inside the orphanages were unaware of the hidden cameras placed within the interviewers clothing. It was obviously true because the video footage was rough and jumpy. You know how you can tell when microphones and cameras are hidden because the video images are jumping around, actually causing you to feel queasy because the image won't stand still? The voices were not clear either. It sounded as if they were inside a tunnel and the voices were slightly muffled with an echoing ring to them. I felt physically nauseous just watching, *but watch, I did.*

The adults working in the orphanage did not speak English. They spoke with the assistance of an interpreter while they led the "undercover" journalists. They were cooperative and even anxious to share as they moved from room to room throughout the orphanage, answering questions and pointing out various children, sharing their individual cases. One child had been there ten years. Another had not spoken a word in two years. Another child couldn't walk. The woman directing the tour continued to expound on the orphan's conditions as they walked from one room to the next. She said they were not able to provide for their medical needs and even if they had the means, they did not have the kind of medical expertise necessary to treat the severe nature of their ailments.

I was captivated with the program. I turned from my paperwork on the table and watched as the stories unfolded. Charlie and Cody sat quietly on the couch with their backs to me, staring at the images on the screen.

The first orphanage was filled with children of all ages. Many of them were lying on cots or sitting inside simple wood framed cribs. Some children were obviously too big to still be in a crib but were kept there anyway. Every room appeared to be overcrowded, poorly furnished and in need of repair. There were no decorations, toys, or play areas. I didn't see anything even remotely similar to what we're used to seeing in child care centers here in America. The children had little clothing on and all were thin and mostly lifeless. The looks on their faces displayed only sadness. Some were crippled and bedridden but could not be moved around due to the lack of wheelchairs. Several children lay listless on beds with no sheets or blankets, and others sat in chairs, doing nothing. It was heart-wrenching to watch. *How can this be real?*

The caregivers described several of the situations that brought these kids to the orphanage. Parents earned very little income and could not provide for themselves, much less their children. Often, children were left at the front door of the orphanage with no information, thus no family to which they could be returned. The orphanage workers were doing the best they could. But sadly, these kids had very little hope for a future inside or outside those walls.

The children peered up at the faces of the strangers walking through the rooms, curiosity in their eyes. It was as if they were hoping someone would pick them up and play with them, hold them or take them away to another place, a place where they would have fun and be loved. Their eyes pleaded, *"I'm here! Are you going to take me with you?"*

The "undercover" journalists continued through the orphanage. They had to do this story "undercover" because of Russia's government. They would have never been allowed to tell the story otherwise. The caregivers wanted to share; they wanted to get the word out—about the dire conditions the orphans endured inside these walls. There was little food, clothing, medicine, or money provided for these children. It seemed their government had abandoned them.

At another orphanage, the children were living in various deteriorating conditions. Older children were working, cleaning and helping to prepare meals for the younger ones. Some were left lying in beds all day with little or no exercise. Several children had already lost the ability to walk because they had been confined to a bed or crib for so long that their legs were deformed and had no muscle development.

As the group walked outside between buildings, there was a little girl sitting all by herself at a crude wooden picnic table. I didn't see any playground equipment. Obviously, she had nothing to do. She was tiny, with thick black hair and had deep pocketed brown eyes. Her tiny frame suggested a girl about three years of age. They said she was actually five! She sat and stared at the entourage walking by. From a distance, one journalist asked about her. She had been there for three years and was in need of a special surgical procedure that would correct a hearing loss. She was now almost completely deaf due to an infection she had while in the orphanage. By the time they had discovered the hearing loss, it was too late to do anything to help her. The resources and medical care needed weren't afforded to orphanages.

I was completely engrossed in the program now. Wow! I couldn't believe the conditions those children were living in. I was sick to my stomach. The little dark-haired five-year old girl just sat there staring up at the people walking nearby with her big, sad eyes, curious why they were there. *So heart wrenching.*

The caregiver explained what happens to children who remain in the orphanage without being adopted or returned to a family member. Upon reaching the age of eighteen, they will have to be sent to one of the many prison facilities or work camps in Russia. This is because they have grown up in this confined and controlled environment, being part of the system. They cannot be released into a society they have never known. The public cannot be expected to take them in and care for them. Their system offered no other options. Some of the luckier, healthier children will be adopted, but most will never be given that opportunity. They will go into the prison system and be put to work. When I heard this, I was shocked!

Tears swelled up, escaping my eyes as I watched. I noticed my husband and son also transfixed to the images on the screen. The program had stirred so many emotions inside me. It all appeared to be sad and hopeless. *How could we live in a world where this was happening? How could children be living like this?*

When the program ended, all three of us sat in silence for several seconds. Then, Cody turned, looked deliberately at me and said, "Hey, why can't we go get one of those kids? We have plenty of food here and an extra bedroom. They could come live with us."

Wow! What a sweet thing to say. I understood what he was feeling. He seemed so sincere. I just smiled at him, not knowing quite what to say. An awkward silence lingered between us. He was still looking at me, waiting for my response. I always have answers for my son, but this? Was this really a serious question? Charlie wasn't looking at me or at Cody for that matter. I hoped he would chime in, say something.... anything......*Come on, Charlie,* **you** *take this one.*

For what seemed an eternity, waiting for Charlie's input and realizing he had nothing to add, I finally said to Cody, "I, uh... don't know." I could see in his eyes he meant what he said. He just stared at me. I found myself unable to respond to his question. What could I say? I was speechless.

Averting his gaze, finally I stood up and walked to the edge of the couch and looked into his eyes and said, "Cody, I know it's really sad how those children are living. We need to pray for them." I looked toward my husband still sitting on the couch and sought his eye contact. *Hey! Help me out here!*

Finally, Charlie said, "It's terrible that they would send them to prison if they never get returned to their family." *Aww, come on Charlie!* Clearly, he was avoiding the question, too.

"Yeah…. I guess they just don't have any other options." I added, hoping to end the conversation.

Cody sat quietly on the couch, waiting for something more from his parents, only to be told by his dad that it was time to get ready for bed. He slowly got up and headed toward the bathroom to brush his teeth, but before he reached his intended destination, Charlie called to him, "Wait a second mister, come give me a hug."

Cody ran to his dad, obliging his request, saying, "Love you, dad."

"Love you too, son. Good night."

My husband continued watching TV while I helped Cody get into bed. We each said a prayer for the children in the orphanages. I hugged him again, repeating how much I loved him. "Good night," I whispered as I closed his bedroom door and went back to the table to try to do some more work—attempting to push the images of those children out of my mind.

That night I had a dream about the petite, dark-haired little girl with the hearing loss. I imagined her being part of our family. She was deaf and I was able to communicate with her in sign language. Our family was happy with the "new addition"…. *in my dream!*

And just like that, God's work had begun. The seed had been planted. I just didn't know it yet.

• • •

*I believe God reveals His plans to us through many means, but we must be willing to yield to His leading and His will. We have to 'die' to ourselves every day in order for Him to be first in our lives; we can't focus on Him until we stop focusing on ourselves. God may reveal His will to us through prayer and seeking Him. He may reveal His will through His word while we are reading. He often uses circumstances and people in our lives to reveal His will to us.*

CHAPTER 4

# That Question

That question! It wouldn't go away. I didn't have an answer. Me! Always the one in control of everything. The diligent manager at work; the primary provider at home; the mother who balanced every area of our lives the best she knew how, now at a loss for words. *"Why can't we get one of those kids?"* *Why would we? A kid in an orphanage in Russia?? It's ridiculous. Our lives are good just the way they are. Why? Why? I don't want to think about it. Stop!*

• • •

I'm reminded of the wisteria that grows along the fence in my neighbor's backyard; a vine with lovely purple blooms that cast off a sweet scent of lilac. I enjoy them during the spring and early summer, but the vines that carry those blooms continue to grow and multiply, devouring anything and everything in their path, making it nearly impossible to get rid of. The pesky vines stretch out across our back gate, weaving themselves in every direction, over and under the fence. I am constantly having to pull them out or cut them back. It's very frustrating.

This is how God begins His work in me, starting with a thought; a small seed, planted in my heart and mind. It sits there, nudging me, taking root—trying to grow. It won't go away. My mind ponders it, mulling it over—around and around, trying to push it aside or perhaps pull it out by its roots, but it continues to grow right back, over and over. I can't get rid of this weed! Only it's not a weed. It's really more like a strange flower, an unknown species I've never seen before. I want to look at it, study it, but I don't know what to do with it. Should I pull it out, push it deeper in the ground, or let it grow and see what it becomes? Will it take over like wisteria?

God is trying to tell me something in this place where I am, but I don't understand. In my simple human mind and heart, I just can't grasp what's happening at the time. So, in this particular case, I decided to bury the seed as deep as possible and hoped it wouldn't grow back. *Just ignore it.*

• • •

The Monday after the orphanage story had aired, I went to work and about my normal daily routine. Even amidst all the work I was doing, images from the *20/20* program continued to creep forward in my mind. I couldn't get Cody's question, 'Why can't we get one of those kids?' out of my head. I had to resolve this somehow. Who could I talk to? I wanted to find someone who would concur that this was all crazy nonsense.

I chose to share with a co-worker in my department. She had not seen the show but listened as I described the poor conditions inside the Russian orphanages. I told her how my son had asked why we couldn't go "get" one of those kids and how I couldn't push the question out of my head because I didn't have an answer. I asked her what she thought. Instead of agreeing with me that it was a foolish idea, she suggested I talk to another employee in our company who had adopted a child from India. *Oh, ok. So you don't think this is crazy?*

I recalled the referenced employee having in the past shared pictures of his adopted daughter from India, but I had never really thought much about his adoption experience until that moment. *Maybe I'll go talk with him later.* I thanked my co-worker for listening and went back to work. God was watering that seed, but I wanted nothing to do with it.

Immediately after our conversation, the question was still there, but I thought I had convinced myself the whole idea was ludicrous. Adoption? I had no idea how it worked. And an adoption of this magnitude was way beyond my comprehension. I had already struggled raising two kids on my own and still had another one at home. Why would I even be considering anything like this? And why could I not stop thinking about that question?

I wasn't yet consciously aware that God had begun a work in me. I kept the seed buried deep inside—at least for a few days.

• • •

*God plants seeds in the gardens of our mind and heart. We are often unaware of the seeds He's planting. We tend to our* mind-gardens ourselves. Normally, we are in complete control of what gets planted and we know what's there. Maybe we hear a word from the pastor—Good one! I'll plant that! Or read a line in a book that makes an impression—Great line! Definitely need to plant those words. Perhaps a trusted friend or relative says something profound—Yes, I want to remember that—-planting... But today, we notice a freshly tilled area of soil in our garden. Where did THAT come from? I know I didn't plant it! Hmmm. Should I take a closer look? Nah. I won't concern myself with it right now. I have other things to do.

God is communicating something to us, but we are either unwilling or not ready to respond. Yes, it's difficult to allow someone else to run things for us. We want to be in control. It's our selfish human nature.

CHAPTER 5

# Who Am I?
# A Look Back

Growing up in a military family and traveling around the world wasn't easy for me or my three younger sisters. We moved around a lot: from Newfoundland, Canada to Washington to Guam to Germany and many more places in between! Finding and keeping friends was the biggest challenge. Sometimes, just when we seemed to be settling in, we would have to move again. Saying goodbye to friends, although heartbreaking, became a normal part of my life. Needless to say, my family became the only constant in my world.

My dad taught me to think for myself. He was the greatest influence in my life, both as a father and leader. During my youth, he wasn't always around. He would often be sent on an assignment somewhere away from where we lived. I relished the time when he was home. I looked up to him. I thought he was the smartest person on the planet. I would often go to him with questions about schoolwork or seek his opinion on a multitude of subjects. I knew he had the answers and great information to share, but he rarely responded with what I wanted. Instead, he would turn my questions back to me, saying, "What do *you* think? How might *you* find that information?" I often left his side feeling frustrated, with my head hung down, yet somehow more determined than ever. This was long before the internet! I had to pull out the encyclopedias or go to the library to find answers!

I grew to be more and more independent. I filled my life with hobbies, including: drawing and painting, playing the piano, sewing, crocheting, reading, and also did as much as I could to help my mom take care of our home and raise my younger sisters. I could have become a loner; instead, I became a leader. I wanted to be just like my dad, holding all the answers.

When I was sixteen, my dad retired from the Air Force after serving twenty years, moving our family to Tulsa, Oklahoma (his childhood home). After finishing college, he started a new career in education. He actually taught at the same high school I attended during my junior and senior years. Unfortunately, I was never in any of his classes. Classmates told me they liked his teaching style and learned a lot from him, especially in History. He taught many subjects to high school students for another twenty years before retiring from his second career.

My mother was always available. She loved being a military mom, traveling with our family to all the places we lived around the world. She worked hard to provide a good home and lots of opportunities for her four girls. While we were growing up, mother loved playing cards and games with us. She was fun to be with and always seemed happy.

I'll never forget how much she enjoyed doing things with her girls, like dressing up at Halloween to surprise trick-or-treaters, building snow animals with us after a big snowfall or singing silly songs to keep us entertained. She even created little games for us to play while we were on road trips, traveling across the states when my dad had received a new assignment. Those trips in the station wagon could be dreadfully long and boring but our mother somehow managed to make them bearable with her fun, challenging games, such as: How many rail cars can you count on the train passing by? How many different state license plates can you identify? My sisters and I would also play the "slug-bug" challenge; see a "slug-bug", call it first, get a point! In case you're wondering, "slug-bugs" were Volkswagen Beetles, which were fairly common during the sixties. If you were lucky, you might spot a "slug-bug bus" (VW van). That earned you double points!

My mother created family "together time" for us. Every year at Christmas time, she baked sugar cookies. My sisters and I would sit around the kitchen table decorating cookies with different colors of icing and sprinkles. She made it fun and didn't seem to mind the big mess we always made. It became one of our family traditions and my favorite time of year.

While living in Tacoma, Washington, at the age of eleven, I found a stray cat hanging around outside our apartment and brought it inside to show my mother. She wasn't so sure about allowing me to keep it, but after my persistent begging and pleading, she gave in. Within a short time, I began itching and having a hard time breathing. Mother said, "You might be allergic to the cat!" I remember crying when I had to let the cat go but soon discovered my mother was right. No more itching. She consoled me the best she could, redirecting me to one of my many other interests like painting, drawing, and eating ice cream, which worked!

Even though I was raised in a military family, moving every few years, making friends, then saying goodbye, I have to say I had a great childhood. Living all over the world afforded me the opportunity to see and experience different cultures and environments, which helped mold me into who I am today. We didn't attend any particular church regularly due to the fact that we moved so often, but we did attend a Christian church whenever we could which provided me with a biblical foundation and moral principles. I was very fortunate to have both my parents always present in my life. I thank God for them.

At the age of seventeen, I met my future husband while attending a vocational school where I learned the basics of my career, graphic design. After high school, he and I continued to see each other even though we both attended separate colleges in different parts of the state. Soon we realized we wanted to be married so we dropped out of college (against the advice of our parents—on both the marriage and dropping out of college). Within a few years, we had two children. We were not prepared and began to grow apart. A few years after that, we divorced. I should have listened to my parents. I blamed myself. I struggled and soon found myself working two and three jobs just to support myself and my children. This was not the life I had imagined.

As if life couldn't get worse, I went through another relationship that I wouldn't wish on anyone. This was physically and mentally abusive. After a tumultuous two years, I called out to God for help and managed to break away. Depressed and alone with my two children, I eventually crawled out of the dark hole I was in—determined to never have another man in my life.

A few years later, in December of 1989, I met Charlie. (Never say never!)

*Now we're caught up.*

## CHAPTER 6

# Seeking Direction

## February, 1999

Several weeks after the airing of the *20/20* episode on Russian orphanages, that seed was well hidden. *Or so I thought.* Then, one afternoon, while doing some designing on my computer at work, the program popped back into my head, for no logical reason. *Now wait a minute, I buried that seed!* I think I had actually hoped it would just wither away on its own. Boy was I wrong. God had a plan and was trying to pull me in. I tried dealing with it myself by not listening to His voice. However, His voice was louder than mine. I was trying to bury that "flower" while He was raising it up and I was losing the battle!

Let's take a breath here. Is God really trying to communicate something to me? I slowed down to consider what was happening. What exactly was God trying to tell me? I'd learned from experience when a thought continually enters my mind, it's often His Holy Spirit speaking to me. Of course, it must be tested. If it's a positive, nurturing thought, it's from God. It has to be something that actually leads me closer to Him, not away from Him. It's His way of trying to teach me something or He just wants me to listen and respond to Him. This is exactly what was happening to me.

Thoughts about adoption kept bombarding my mind. I would try to focus on my tasks at work, but my mind would drift off to questions about adoption. *Focus! Stop thinking about it. Get back to work. Keep yourself on track. Children. Orphans. Adoption? Get out of my head!* I could not stop thinking about those children. I'm going to explode!

•  •  •

*Faith is believing in something we cannot see. It is following what's leading our heart without knowing why, but trusting anyway.*

•  •  •

In mid-February, 1999, I conceded to God's plan, having no idea what would happen next. Out loud (in my mind) I said, "Ok, God! If you want me to look into adoption, I will!" Instantly, I had a sense of peace. My mind focused. I felt as if angels were taking both of my hands into theirs and saying, "We're here. Don't worry. We're holding you and won't let go."

I had not yet even spoken of any of this with my husband. Can you believe it? I'd been dealing with all of this on my own. I was convinced all these thoughts would eventually go away, but now I knew for sure they weren't going anywhere. I realized I had to talk to Charlie before I did anything else. That night, after dinner, I shared with him what had been happening to me ever since the *20/20* episode and Cody's question. He patiently listened as I explained the mental turmoil I was going through. To my surprise, he said he knew I was going through something but just didn't know what it was. He told me he trusted me and said, "If God wants us to adopt a child, I'm fine with that."

Wow! I was surprised at his response. He didn't have a problem with us adopting a child? *Was God working on him, too?*

"I'm not sure about anything at this point," I continued, "I have to get more information. I'll figure out what to do."

"Ok. Let me know if you need my help," he replied. And that was it. That was how Charlie was. He trusted me to make good decisions, especially when God was directing me. He knew I would dig deep and gather all the information before presenting my findings to him so we could discuss the next steps.

At work the next day, I asked God, "Ok, Lord. So now what? Where do I begin? What do you want me to do?" Where did it all start? I'm listening. Yes, the program, *20/20*. Maybe they have information on the internet. How do I find their website? I was reminded of the training I received from my dad as a child. I had to find answers for myself, one way or another. At least we now had the internet. What a wonderful source of information! Right there at my fingertips. I wouldn't stop until I had answers. *I will get this over with once and for all!*

I sat at my computer, opened the Internet and the search engine we typically used in our company. I typed in the search line *20/20*. Seemed straight forward to me. Too simple, actually.

I secretly hoped it would be much more difficult. *I had barely started and was already beginning to fight God again!*

Sure enough, *20/20* popped up at the top of the list of search results. I clicked on the link and was taken to their website. I saw a box to enter more search words and typed: Russian Orphanages. Wow! The entire transcript came right up! Instantly! There it was, in black & white, on my computer screen. *Oh no!*

. . .

*When God is telling you to do something or leading you through a situation, He will help you every step of the way, IF you let Him. The important thing is, IF. Should you choose to fight Him on it, then it will become a battle and guess who's gonna be miserable?*

. . .

I proceeded to read the story online, scanning the text for a contact person's name or a phone number I could call to get more information. *I'll just scroll down and probably won't find anything.* What in the world would I say even if I did find a number to actually call and talk to someone? Scrolling…scrolling…wouldn't you know, there *was* a phone number! *Right, God. Ok, I'll call.*

A man answered the phone, introduced himself, and I asked, "How do I find out about possibly adopting a child from one of the Russian orphanages that was shown on the *20/20* program that aired a few weeks ago?" He said he knew about the program and put me on hold. I waited several minutes, almost hanging up, thinking I didn't want to find out. When he returned he said there was another office handling this information so he transferred me to that office. I already felt uncomfortable wondering why it took so long for him to return to the line.

Another man's voice came on the line so I asked him the same question. He hesitated a moment, sighed and said he understood what I needed, but he couldn't help me. Another hesitation... so, I asked who *could* help me.

"Is there someone else I can talk to?" I asked, explaining how I might want to adopt one particular little girl I had seen in one of the orphanages. I smiled in my mind, envisioning that little dark-eyed five year old girl with the hearing loss.

He replied, "No. There is no one else you can talk to." It was a flat out, blunt rejection. I felt as if I had hit a dead end so quickly! A door slamming in my face.

Then his tone changed, a little more sympathetic, as he continued, "Look, I know what you are trying to do is really commendable and I wish I could give you more information, but, in fact, we were in there undercover, so we are not *allowwwwed* to share anything (I visualized him doing air quotes around *allowed*). I wish we could help you. I'm really sorry."

I was shocked, but, it did make sense, still...I really thought I could get **something**, possibly a name or address of someone who was actually working with Americans who wanted to adopt or send money...something...**anything**. *Is that what I needed to say?*

I asked him if there was anything else I could do to get more information. He suggested that I contact the Bureau of Consular Affairs in Washington, D.C. He laughed and said, "But you will never be able to find a particular child you saw on that airing of *20/20* no matter what you do." Then he hung up. And I hung up......*crushed. God, this is too much for me!* An agency in Washington D.C.? *No way.*

I felt beaten and overcome with disappointment. I sat there awhile thinking about whether I should just forget the whole thing or try to find this "agency" in Washington. Just the name of the organization overwhelmed me. It was located in Washington D.C.! *Think. Think. My dad saying, 'figure it out.' Where can you go to get more information?* Maybe there was a local agency I could find that could answer my questions.

Just then I remembered the co-worker who had adopted a baby from India. *This is a good time to go talk to him.* I sought him out. I asked him exactly how he adopted his little girl. I shared my *20/20* experience with him, explaining how I was considering the possibility of adopting a child from a Russian orphanage. *There it was. I had actually said it OUT LOUD!*

NOW, I want to make it clear that even though I had reached out to others for information, I was still conversing in such a way to convince myself that I couldn't do this. I wanted road blocks. I wanted doors to shut. I wanted to get on with my comfortable life and forget all of this! I had to stop thinking about what *I wanted.* When I allowed God to be in control, He continued to open the doors and remove the road blocks. He never said it would be easy or even make sense. I just had to trust Him to lead me through and put Him first. I needed more faith!

The co-worker proceeded to share his story with me. He told me about the agency he and his wife had used for their adoption that was right here in Tulsa. He then gave me the name of the lady that handled Russian adoptions and... you guessed it... her phone number. Once again, I had no excuse. I only had to pick up the phone. Can't get much easier, can it?

• • •

*When you follow God's will for your life, you will find answers and directions. But sometimes we just don't want them! Or, we feel uncertain and scared. It's perfectly normal to feel that way. God's way may often seem totally illogical within our human understanding. He will equip you with the tools you need to do the task. But you do have to reach out and take them.*

• • •

I waited until I had a few minutes of free time at work, then placed the call. The adoption agency was Dillon International, located in midtown Tulsa. The receptionist answered and connected me to Barbara, the coordinator for Russian adoptions.

This is the gist of the conversation:

"Hello. I want to get some information about possibly adopting a child that's in an orphanage in Russia. Are you the one I need to talk to?" I asked.

"Yes," she answered. "Exactly what did you want to know?"

"Well, this may seem strange, but my husband and I watched a *20/20* program on TV recently about Russian orphanages and we saw this five-year old girl that we were interested in locating and possibly adopting," I said.

"Oh," she replied, "yes, I know the program you're talking about, but it's not that easy. Actually, what you're asking is impossible. Let me ask you why you think you want to adopt?"

I was a little intimidated and didn't know what to say. "Well," I said, "I just want to get some information. I'd like to know how this all works."

"Sounds like you just feel sorry for those children and aren't really serious about adoption, much less adopting from Russia." Then she added, "I suggest you forget about this. It's not for you."

I was stunned by her dismissive tone. Isn't she the least bit interested in finding adoptive parents? I paused a moment, considering what she just said, thinking maybe she's right. I replied, "Oh, ok, thanks." I hung up. I immediately felt the tears coming. Flushed, embarrassed. Wow! What just happened? Am I going to cry? Did she really say that? How dare her! All I wanted was some information. Why did she brush me off like that?

I sat there several minutes, feeling defeated, wondering what to do next. What in the world *was* I doing? This lady was right! Thinking we could actually adopt a child from Russia was ridiculous. She was right to tell me to forget about it. *Get rid of that flower! Pull it out by the roots! It doesn't belong in my mind-garden.*

My emotions were taking over. I wanted to call her back and give her a word or two! But, I knew ranting would be the wrong thing to do right now. I calmed myself by sitting and thinking quietly. I pondered what to do. I felt beaten—more determined to end this whole thing. *Now what, Lord?* Maybe I should let it rest a day or two to see what happens. I'll talk to Charlie about everything and see what he thinks.

Later that evening, I shared with my husband what had happened. He offered to call her back himself, but I told him I would call back the next day and set an appointment to go in and talk face to face. We both felt that would be best. If God was closing a door, we would soon know.

The next day I called back to speak to Barbara again. This time she was very friendly and accommodating on the phone. *Hmmm, strange.* It was as if she were a different person. Was this God's way of saying, *everything is in my control and I want you to proceed?*

She apologized for the way she had responded to me on the previous days' call. She said she just wanted me to make sure this was something I really wanted to pursue. She further explained it was her way of "weeding out" those who really aren't serious about adopting. *Ok, I can accept that.* She asked when we'd like to come in. I looked at my calendar and while I was doing that, she asked if March 5th was a good day to meet. I smiled because March 5th is my birthday. What could be more perfect than meeting on my birthday? *Was this more confirmation?* I set the appointment for 11 a.m., assuming Charlie and I could go to lunch afterward to celebrate my birthday. I had already planned to take off work that day anyway. It was just a week away.

# CHAPTER 7

# Dillon
# International

## March, 1999

Charlie and I drove to Dillon International to meet with Barbara on March 5th, 1999. I had written down some questions and possible obstacles that I felt might prevent us from adopting a child from Russia. *Pushing that flower down again.....* Were we too old to adopt? I had just turned forty-two and my husband was five years older than me. What would we find out? The prospect of adoption felt exciting, yet daunting at the same time. I tried to keep my mind open to whatever we would learn. Would this day mark the beginning of something huge? We would just have to trust God. After all, He had led us this far, right? *Right!*

The agency was smaller than what I had expected. There were only a few offices with a modest size reception area. While waiting for Barbara, I noticed a couple of glass enclosed displays mounted on the wall with collections of items from various foreign countries. There were framed photographs of children of various ages with adoptive families, mostly children from China, but another display held photos of adoptees from Russia, India and other countries. Despite the small office space, it appeared quite a few children had been adopted through this agency.

Barbara appeared, introduced herself and led us to a table down the hall where we all sat, beginning with small talk. Still apprehensive after our first telephone conversation, I was unsure what to expect, but soon her amiable, motherly demeanor put my mind at ease. She asked why we were considering adoption. I proceeded to explain how we had seen the *20/20* program about children in orphanages in Russia and how our son had asked us afterward, "Why can't we go get one of those kids?"

Charlie added, "Yeah, they even said if kids grow up in the orphanage, they have to go to a prison or work camp when they turn eighteen. I couldn't believe it."

I told her how God kept impressing on me to look into adoption and how I felt He was telling us to adopt a child from Russia, maybe even try to locate that little girl with the hearing loss. I explained that neither Charlie nor I had ever dreamed of adopting a child. I thought she must surely think we are crazy. Instead, she smiled and said, "God works in mysterious ways." *He does indeed.*

We each shared stories about our families. She told us all about Dillon International, how it began and how she became involved. She had adopted children internationally herself and intended to adopt more in the future. I felt like a sponge, absorbing every word she spoke. I wanted to know everything. I needed to hear about the entire process of foreign adoption. Listening intently, feeling more and more overwhelmed, somehow—in ways I can't explain—I felt more convinced than ever that we were supposed to begin the process.

She led us into her office to get some paperwork. Charlie and I sat down as she handed us a printout of the Dillon adoption procedures, including a list of countries with which they were associated. She smiled and asked us if we would consider adopting a child from Ukraine instead of Russia. I looked at my husband and he raised his eyebrows as if to say, *"Don't look at me."*

I shrugged and said, "Well, we really feel like we're supposed to adopt from Russia, you know, the program?" Then, I asked, "Why Ukraine?"

Barbara's eyes lit up as she happily expounded on how Ukraine had recently "opened up," allowing Americans to adopt and that there were many girls available for adoption. She explained Ukraine was comprised mostly of Russian people, having formerly been part of the Soviet Union. The adoption process was very similar for both countries. She said Russia, however, was the most expensive country from which to adopt children. I was clueless so I asked what she meant by, "opened up" recently. She explained that Ukraine had not been allowing Americans to adopt their orphans due to some diplomatic issues. Some kind of rule changes had taken place. They had only recently begun allowing Americans in again. Barbara was very proud to share that Dillon had just completed their first adoption from Ukraine to an Oklahoma couple a few months earlier. I looked at my husband and we both agreed it seemed like a good option for us; however,

I wanted to make sure this was the direction God wanted us to go. I told her we would pray about it.

Barbara, practically our best friend now, shared with us some of the documents we would be dealing with should we choose to move forward: Children Available for Adoption, Estimated Time for Adoption Process, Steps Involved in the Adoption Process, Dillon Policies Regarding Applicants, Immigration and Naturalization (INS) Policies, Individual Country Requirements, Health Requirements, and Adoption Expenses by Country. Ultimately, she handed us a Fee Schedule for Ukrainian adoptions.

We didn't spend too much time looking over the paperwork in her office. Instead, Barbara told us we could take as much time as we wanted. She described how some couples take up to three years to complete the adoption while others finish in less than a year. Each adoption was an individual process. Every couple handled it differently. We felt no pressure whatsoever. We could go at our own pace and pay for each step as we wanted or when money was available. She told us Dillon was there to support us in any way they could. If we wanted to proceed quickly, we could. If we chose to take it one step at a time, wait, then move ahead, we could do that as well. She said it was up to us.

The meeting was coming to a close and Barbara asked if we had any other questions. We didn't at that time. She recommended we look over the paperwork and call back when we were ready to begin. As we were about to leave, she smiled and said, "I hope you will decide to adopt from Ukraine."

Charlie and I left Dillon, going to lunch as planned. We chatted about the meeting and how God was working in our lives.

Charlie said, "We should get a girl. I'm sure you'd like to have another daughter to raise."

"Really?" I responded, "You know if this actually happens, I still have the name, Shelby, picked out."

He replied, "Sounds good to me!"

I was happy just thinking of it, but I still didn't know if this was truly God's plan. We chatted about Ukraine. Neither of us were even sure where Ukraine was. I'd never heard much about it. We agreed we needed to find out more about this country. I also wanted to make sure adopting from Ukraine, instead of Russia, was God's will.

That night, I prayed, asking God if we were doing the right thing. Did He want us to adopt a little girl from Ukraine? I had a sense of peace, at that time, about the situation. I hear people say, "It just felt right." For me, it was more of a spiritual confirmation, of accepting God's will. I had no fear of moving into the unknown. *I was ready to allow that strange flower to take root. I was turning over MY way to God's way. My faith was growing.*

• • •

Often, when I wonder if I am doing God's will, He will reassure me through prayer and reading His word. He knows where I am and begins to take over. I don't need to say anything at all. I am given a sense of peace and assurance. That's His way of telling me I am doing the right thing.

I believed He had given me His answer.

This was the first time I began to say a new prayer that would continue over the next several months. My new prayer went something like this:

*"Lord, show us who this little girl is. Touch her heart and let her know that she is special and that we are coming to get her very soon. Protect her and cradle her in your arms for us until we get there. Thank you, Lord."*

• • •

We were ready to proceed but wondered how we could afford it. Paying for something like this really hadn't crossed my mind at all until now. After all, this was all God's doing. He had to provide, right? I saw what the costs were because Dillon had presented us with a comprehensive list of all the expenses involved. At some point, I actually told myself (or maybe God was telling me) not to dwell on any of the costs. Barbara had been very clear on moving at a pace we felt comfortable with and focusing on one step at a time so we wouldn't become overwhelmed. She said we could pause the process if the expenses were too great and then just let her know when we were ready to continue. I never felt pressured as we proceeded.

Charlie and I considered all of our options for ways to come up with money. We had no savings, but I did have a 401K at work. I didn't know if I could get money from my 401K, but found out adoption was listed as one of the approved withdrawals. We discussed taking all the money available and agreed to do that. I had $8000 available for withdrawal, not nearly enough, but a good start.

Another option was to take all the cash we had accrued in our life insurance policies. We each had built up some money in our policies, so we decided to request the money as loans. Those loans amounted to around $6000 and would have to be paid back eventually, but we were glad to have that option.

Those two options were the only ones we had as sources of additional funds other than our regular income. Together, they were still not enough. We would need to come up with another $10,000! Wow! Where will that come from? How would we ever be able to pay for this? And what happens if we start putting money into this process and then find we can't afford to continue? Will we get our money back? Should I even be thinking about it? Or do I just need to believe that God will provide?

• • •

*If we allow God to hold us by the hand and take the lead, we become like a child, holding on tight to our Father's hand—following along. We believe that He knows the way and won't lead us astray, so we actually don't need to concern ourselves with how we're going to get there. We must learn how to trust Him—have faith. He was leading and I trusted Him to provide. If this truly was His will for us, I knew He would pave the way and provide the means.*

• • •

However, I am human. I still wondered how we were going to get the money. God wasn't going to just drop bags of cash on our doorstep. I reminded myself of the fact that Barbara said we could stop at any time and wait until we could pay for the next step in the process. But what if it takes years? The older we get, the less chance we might have to adopt. I just have to allow God to work it all out. *Have faith!*

It's amazing, as I look back now, at how He *did* provide and I don't think I'll ever fully understand how He did it!

# CHAPTER 8

# Family Meeting

## Late March, 1999

We had no clue what we were getting into. Neither of us had ever dreamed of adopting a child, much less one from a foreign country. We literally trusted God with the entire process. Up to this point, He was clearly leading us every step of the way. This was a journey for us and we didn't know what would happen. Our lives were headed in a new direction. I was scared and excited to see how God was going to use us. We were holding His hand. He kept whispering, *"You're in my care now. Come on. I'll show you the way."*

We read through all the paperwork and requirements for international adoption: the fee schedule, initial application and home study, dossier, acceptance and assignment of child, travel information and on and on. Comprehending the vast amount of information we had to read was overwhelming. Breaking it down into smaller pieces made it easier for us to deal with. Each step of the process became a complete and separate objective on which to focus. This allowed us to feel successful after the completion of each one. In other words, once we had accomplished one big task, we could take a little time and when we were ready, move on to the next.

The first official document we signed was an agreement with Dillon International that ended with this statement: [We, the undersigned, acknowledge that we have been informed of the schedule of fees to be paid to Dillon International during the steps of the adoption process.......dated March 21. 1999.] This was just the first of many documents we would sign over the next several months. *Ok, God. We're trusting you to provide.*

So, it's formalized! We are adopting a child from an orphanage in Ukraine. We had no idea how long it might take, but both of us were confident it was going to happen. *This is crazy! What are we getting into?*

Once we made the decision to adopt, we knew we had to share this with our extended family. I called my parents and my sisters and asked them to come over for a "family meeting" at our house. I told them we had something important to share with them. My husband's parents were no longer living and his siblings did not live near us. Charlie said he would call his siblings later to explain what we were doing. I would also have to call my youngest sister who resided in Florida. Family meetings were rare and always meant something big had happened or was about to happen. I can't imagine what my family members must have been thinking.

The next evening, my parents, my younger single sister, my second sister and her husband and daughter, all came to our house for what was a seldom held, but highly anticipated, family meeting. Everyone gathered, sitting together in our living room.

I felt nervous about exactly how to share this life-changing decision with my family. I didn't know what sort of reaction we would get. Would they even understand or think we had lost our minds? Would they try to convince us not to do it or embrace us? Whatever they might offer, in the way of opinions, meant a great deal to me. I wanted more than anything for them to embrace it with us. I prayed they would listen and accept what we were doing as a good thing and understand this was what God was calling us to do.

I decided the best way to begin was to just come right out and make the announcement. "We are going to adopt a child from Ukraine." I explained how it had all started with us watching the *20/20* program, followed by Cody's question and finally, how we felt this was what God wanted us to do.

Everyone sat silent for what seemed like an eternity. Finally, looking around the room, I asked, "So, what do you think?" I looked from face to face, trying to imagine what they must be thinking. My married sister spoke first. I'll never forget what she said.

"You mean a *real* child?" she asked. She seemed serious and I was perplexed.

I laughed and said, "Well, yes, what did you think we meant?"

She replied that she didn't realize we meant we were actually going to adopt a real child. She said she thought we were talking about one of those "Adopt-a-Child" programs where people send money in return for a bio and photo.

"No," I added, "we actually mean a REAL child."

My mom said she didn't know what to think. She was mostly quiet. Maybe she was still confused and didn't yet understand what we were saying, but I sensed she didn't approve.

Then my dad spoke, "I think it's wonderful! If I were fifteen years younger, I would have loved to have done the same thing." I could see in his eyes that he understood. Having my dad's blessing was a huge relief.

Once the family understood this was really going to happen, they embraced us. Lots of questions ensued but we didn't have many answers. All we could tell them was we would just see what happened in the days and months to come. Knowing we had my family's support felt empowering. Perhaps God had prepared their hearts ahead of time.

Later that same day, as I reflected on the family visit, I replayed in my mind what my dad had said; that he would have loved to adopt a child if he were fifteen years younger. Was he serious? I suppose he would have gotten that boy he'd never had. Made sense. But it also provided me with the support I needed. My dad's opinion was very important to me. With his stamp of approval, moving forward was so much easier. I felt like a heavy rock had been lifted off my shoulders. This was the beginning of our adoption journey. We had accepted God's will. We're going to do this!

• • •

*When God tells us to do something, we really don't need anyone else's approval. However, having their approval makes things less stressful. After all, we are only human. We all have family. We want those that are closest to us to believe in us and approve of what we do. We want their support. We all make decisions every day and don't always seek God's guidance when we should. Yet, He continues to love us even though we often disappoint Him. His grace is amazing.*

CHAPTER 9

# The Process

## April, 1999

The paperwork we would face over the next several months was mind-boggling, but the assistance and support we received from the staff of Dillon International helped tremendously. They explained each part of the process in detail, using simple, understandable language that made us feel very comfortable. Charlie and I were reassured that we could pause at any point when we might want to take a break or just needed more time. It didn't matter where we were in the process. The staff at Dillon were always encouraging.

The first thing we were required to do was attend an adoption workshop. Dillon periodically invited families who had completed their adoptions to come and share their experience with couples beginning their adoption journeys. The workshop we attended was not only informative, but allowed us the opportunity to meet others beginning the process as well as families in the post-adoption phase.

At the workshop were newly adopted children from various countries. One particular little girl adopted from China made quite an impression on me. She was six years old and very brave, displaying confidence as she shared "her story" with all the families in attendance. She told everyone how she had been abandoned by her birth mother at a bus station and someone from a local hospital found her and took her to the hospital. Luckily she went to an orphanage where she dreamed about finding a new family to love. An American couple chose to adopt her and brought her to America. She exuded happiness as she described living with her new family!

I sat in awe listening to her speak, surprised at how articulate she was. I was impressed, not only by the fact that she didn't seem nervous standing up in front of a group of about fifty people, but about the fact that she knew "her story." At that moment, I knew it would be important for our little girl to know "her story" too, especially the part about how she was chosen by God to be in our family.

A few days after the workshop, a woman from Dillon came to our home. If I had a fourth sister, it would have been Maren. She was smart, warm, and easy-going. She told us she was responsible for building our "dossier" that would eventually be sent to the adoptive country to review and ultimately approve. While we listened to her describe her role at Dillon, I felt like I'd known her all my life. I trusted her completely.

Maren began to lay out the "dossier" beginning with the home study which consisted of interviews and photos of our home. We were required to show how we lived and provided for our family, and that we had the means and space to accommodate another child. Three home studies would eventually be completed before the process was finalized. The first was called the pre-adoption study or interview; the second—the process (means), and the third was the post-adoption study (placement evaluation). Each of these were spaced several months apart. Maren made it all sound simple.

The interview consisted of questions reaching into every aspect of our lives. Where do you work? How long have you been there? Will you continue to work after the adoption? How will the child be cared for? Do you attend church and for how long? Will you continue to go to church with your adopted child? Where will the child sleep? Do you have a separate room for her? Maren was very kind and patient, answering every question she could. She spent about an hour in our home during the first visit and left us with more papers to review.

Next, we had to submit photos of our home, inside and out. Each room had to be photographed. We needed to show we had a bedroom for another child. Photographing that room wasn't easy as we had been using it as the "bonus" room—accumulating stuff for quite a while. Normally, I would keep things clean and orderly, but now it was time to declutter the entire house!

Charlie and I were each required to write separate, personal letters explaining why we wished to adopt a child, using our own words, in our own handwriting. We were not supposed to share what we'd written with each other. *Why not?* I had to stop and ask myself how to write that letter, since it wasn't my idea or my husband's idea to adopt. Neither of us had ever thought about adopting a child. This was God's plan. I knew this letter would be part of our dossier, ultimately sent to Ukraine for review and would influence their decision to accept us as adoptive parents. So, what should I say and how do I say it?

Writing the letter was awkward. I had to put into writing why I wanted to adopt a child. I had a choice to make. I could have said it was *my* decision or *our* decision or maybe because we were now too old or I was unable to have another biological child. Those were all good reasons that most people might use, but not true in our case. I had to somehow put into words what seemed illogical to me. How would someone else understand this? How do I explain this was all about following God's will and having complete faith in His leading? I knew God was in complete control of this entire adoption and He would take care of everything. Somehow I had to get that across and have it make sense. I had to be truthful, so I told "the story" in my letter, and then we each gave our letters to Maren. Charlie and I did as we were instructed and didn't tell each other what we'd written.

Dillon asked us to provide them with three references of people other than family members. They sent those referenced people requests for letters of recommendation. Those people were required to also send hand-written letters to Dillon, telling why they thought we would be good parents. Charlie and I never knew what they wrote.

Together, we went through the checklist for our home study requirements, making sure we had everything completed and then followed up with Maren for review. By mid-April we were about one-fourth of the way through the process.

Maren handed us a lengthy form that listed various items and conditions we would deem acceptable in a child we chose to adopt. Each item required a Yes or No response and some asked for explanation to our response. Many of those questions were very difficult to answer. Would you be willing to accept a child with a disorder? What type of disorder? Would you accept a child with a disease? An abnormality? Abused? Drug-addicted? Fetal alcohol syndrome? The checklist included health-related questions about the birth mother and father too. Of all the questions, the easiest was first—boy or girl? Girl! One item checked off the list, 49 more to go! *Ugh.* Last was the child's age.

We really hadn't considered what age child we should adopt. I didn't know what God had in mind for us. I knew I didn't want a baby, but I also didn't think we should get an older child, so, perhaps a toddler? What did Cody think? Did he want a sister that was close to his age or much younger? We asked him and he said he didn't care but that he just didn't want a baby. He thought it would be nice to have a sibling he could play with, somewhat closer to his age.

I spoke with Barbara, asking her at what age children were the most difficult to place in an adoptive family. In other words, I felt strongly we should choose a child who was less likely to be adopted. This is what God had revealed to me. It came from the *20/20* story of how older children are much less likely to be adopted. Barbara said most adoptive families want newborns, explaining when children reach the age of two, they are much less likely to be placed in a family. So, we decided on a child between two and four years old.

We carefully considered each entry on the checklist, marking "yes" to the physical conditions we were willing to accept. Stopping to consider each item was time consuming! I had no idea there were so many medical conditions to consider in choosing a child, but we concluded if there was anything wrong with the child's health, surely our family physician would be able to address it. Barbara then said we may be informed the child has a serious health issue. "What do you mean?" I inquired.

She said, "You'll likely be told that the child needs surgery or medications only available in America. So don't be surprised if that comes up."

"Wow! How will we know for sure?" I asked.

She responded, "Well, it's highly unlikely to be anything serious. That's how they justify allowing a child to be adopted by Americans."

That's a little scary! Are we going to a country that doesn't want us there? Again, I reminded myself God was in control. If the child has a serious health issue, we would deal with it.

Next, Charlie and I had to complete our own health checklists! We learned every country had its own guidelines and specific requirements. Applicants must be in good mental, emotional, and physical health with no serious illnesses of a life-threatening nature. Prospective parents must be in a specific age and weight range. I was surprised to find out the vast differences in guidelines between countries. At least Ukraine allowed adults up to age forty-nine. Some countries did not.

We were given a chart showing the acceptable height and weight range for men and women. They must not be more than thirty percent overweight. I knew I could shed a few pounds, whereas Charlie could add a few. I hoped we fell within the acceptable range. We both had to have a physical with the doctor's report forwarded directly to Dillon to be added to our dossier.

International adoption policies were next. Couples must have been married for at least three years. *No problem there.* Prior country approval was needed for persons having had more than one previous marriage. *Oops.* We had to produce our previous marriage licenses and divorce records. Luckily, I had copies of my records, but my husband didn't. That meant having to go downtown and locate those records at the court house. One of Charlie's records had been moved to another location in another city! Why, I don't know. We had to take off work, travel to another city and spend a full day in the public records office in order to locate his file, which we finally did.

There were so many requirements. Couples must earn a combined minimum annual salary of $40,000. Our income was over that amount. We had to have health insurance and life insurance. At least one of us had to be a U.S. citizen, currently living in the United States. *Seems peculiar.* Where else would we be living? Perhaps some American citizens residing overseas might not be able to adopt an international child. I really didn't know. We were required to submit our fingerprints and have criminal background checks completed. Last, but not least, Ukraine had its own specific requirements. Applicants must be between twenty-five and forty-nine years old. Preference was given to Christian families! Yay! We met all the requirements! Was there ever any real doubt? *God would not have brought us into this if we were not qualified for the task.*

All documents took time to process at the various agencies involved. And we had to physically be there to make the requests, sign papers, make payments, etc. That meant we had to miss work, which meant lost income. Each process required more money. We were either busy doing paperwork or waiting for paperwork to be processed and returned. Weeks passed as each step was accomplished. In late summer, we had to travel to our state capitol building in Oklahoma City to have documents signed, copied, notarized and filed with the Secretary of State's office.

After all the requirements were complete, we met one more time with Dillon to have everything reviewed, compiled and then forwarded to Washington, D.C. We were told, once D.C. approved, it would be mailed to Ukraine for their review and approval. Dillon said this final process could take up to six months. It was now August, 1999.

*Six months! Finally, we could relax and prepare.*

# CHAPTER 10

# Remodeling

## Summer, 1999

In June, Charlie and I discussed the need to convert our third bedroom, which up until that time had been used as an office-slash-sewing room-slash-exercise room-slash-junk room, back into an actual bedroom for our soon-to-be adopted daughter. It was all beginning to sink in now, becoming more and more real each day. We really are going to adopt a little girl! No longer, "Should we do this or not," but "We **are** doing this!"

We were acutely aware of being in the middle of a huge life change and WE were NOT in control. Terrifying! We had turned it all over to God, not knowing what would happen from one day to the next. Our lives were in turmoil! The smallest decisions seemed to create huge challenges. Charlie and I were arguing about each and every decision to be made. We need an office. Where am I going to put my sewing tables? What about this desk? Where should we put these shelves? We need to get a bed and dresser and rocking chair and clothing and probably should paint this room and... How are we going to make this work? Where's the money going to come from? All the changes were stressful for each of us. *I blamed myself for getting us into this mess even though I knew with all my heart that God was in charge.*

Charlie came up with the idea of closing in our back patio and turning it into an office. Brilliant! *Wait, wait, wait... that's going to require money.* We had both agreed to save every extra dollar for the adoption. At every turn, we were faced with the issue of money. We can't go out to eat. You can't go rent that movie. I can't buy that outfit. Cody can wait on those new shoes. Replacing that chair can wait, too. Paint? Forget that. Save, save, save! We wanted to have money ready for the next step in the process. We still had to come up with another $10,000! An extra room sounded great, but how could we afford it?

During early summer, we noticed an unusual increase in the amount of work Charlie was getting. Jobs were scheduled well into the summer months, among which were several home remodels. That meant he would have materials left over after the jobs were completed. Instead of hauling them to the dump as he would normally do, he could use the materials to build the room enclosure. *God's provision or pure coincidence?*

As materials became available, Charlie started the work of closing in our back patio, changing it into an office. He worked all day on customer's jobs and would come home late, then go out to the patio room and often work well into the night. I worried about him, but he never complained. I was also putting in long hours at my job. I tried to get home before dinner each day so I could help out with Cody or whatever Charlie might need. I was exhausted and on edge. Doubts were settling in again. Would we be able to continue the adoption process? Maybe we should call the whole thing off. I knew I was just tired and feeling overwhelmed! I needed some rest. We all did. *God, what are we doing?*

The summer months flew by. One Saturday morning in early September, as Charlie was laboring on the patio conversion, I decided to venture into the unfinished room to evaluate the progress. Floors were partially completed and the walls were framed, but there was a lot left to do. Charlie asked my opinion about one area in the corner of the room where he wanted to add some shelves in a narrow space. I didn't think it was such a good idea. Without thinking, I injected my opinion, telling him I thought the floor joists were too far apart, the ceiling tiles should be replaced, and that small space would not work for shelves. He thought differently and we began to argue. I'm stressed about work. I'm stressed about money. I'm stressed about the adoption. Everything is beginning to look impossible.

I'm arguing with my husband about the floor spacing when he raised his voice and said, "Trust me! I've been doing this a long time. It will all look great in the end."

"I thought you wanted my input," I yelled. "I'm sorry I said anything!" I immediately regretted what I'd said.

Practically breaking down right there, I managed to pull myself from the room only to run to the bathroom off our master bedroom at the back of the house, closing the door behind me. I leaned over the sink, crying out, "God, what are we doing!? I'm arguing with Charlie. I'm upset with myself for arguing. We're exhausted. You wanted us to do all of this and now we don't have time for each other or money to continue. I want to know if we're doing the right thing, God! I need to know! I want to know something TODAY! Please, Lord!"

I washed my face, calmed my mind, went into the bedroom, sat on the edge of our bed and cried some more. We'd been doing everything God had asked us to do. Now we were in limbo just waiting to hear something from Ukraine which might be months away. I sat quietly for a while, just waiting and listening.

God's reassurance swept over me. *"Be patient. Yes, you have done everything I've asked of you. Remember all of what you've accomplished. Look at how far you've come. I am still leading and in control. Trust me. I am with you."*

A short time later, after gathering myself, I walked down to the mailbox at the front curb of our house to get our mail. As I slowly walked back toward the front door, carrying several pieces of mail, I flipped through the envelopes, scanning what was junk and what wasn't. I pulled out a larger envelope and saw a foreign return address stamped in the upper left corner. *Whoa! What was this?* I kept it in my hand and hurried back inside. It's something from Kiev, Ukraine. I tossed the rest of the mail on the kitchen counter, sat down at the dining room table and tore the envelope open.

I silently began to read the official looking letter with a fancy stamp at the top,

> *Dear Mr. and Mrs. Potter,*
> *We are pleased to inform you that*
> *we have reviewed your dossier*
> *and have approved you for adoption in Ukraine.....*

I paused—chills running up and down my entire body. "CHARLIE!!" I yelled out to the room remodel where he was working.

Charlie rushed in. "What's wrong? Are you ok?"

"It's here! The acceptance letter arrived! From Ukraine! We've been approved!" I continued, "Sit down, let's read it together."

I held the letter in front of us and read the entire thing out loud. At the end of the letter, we were given a date to appear at the adoption center in Kiev.

*You are invited to appear at the Ministry of Adoption Office in Kiev, Ukraine, on November 10th, 1999.*

It was the answer from my desperate plea to God! WOW! He answered my prayer. We ARE doing the right thing! I began to laugh and cry and shout at the same time, "God, You are AWESOME!"

I explained to Charlie how upset I'd been earlier and how I told God I needed confirmation today! Charlie was amazed at how God was working in my life. He hugged me and said, "I better get back to work, huh!"

• • •

*God is truly amazing. He knew exactly where I was and He heard my cry. He knew I needed confirmation and comfort and provided it!*

# CHAPTER 11

# Final Preparations

## Fall, 1999

The letter laid out all the requirements to finalize the adoption along with instructions for our trip including additional documents we would need to bring with us to Ukraine. We called Barbara and scheduled a meeting to discuss the next steps prior to going to Ukraine. We began to feel somewhat anxious as the time grew nearer to our departure date. We still had so much left to do!

Charlie and I really wanted to take Cody with us, but Dillon explained how difficult the trip would be for a young child. They discouraged anyone from taking children with them. We were told about the living arrangements, environment and culture being extremely different to what we are used to in America. Children, especially those under twelve, would find it nearly impossible to adjust. They didn't tell us we *couldn't* take him but strongly advised it would not be a good idea. So we decided to follow their advice. Cody would stay with my parents while we were gone. He didn't mind. He loved his grandparents and knew he'd have a good time with them.

Dillon assisted us with booking all our flights, including our return flights from Kiev and finally, Warsaw, Poland. There was no problem getting there with just two of us, but we had to purchase a third ticket for our return with the adopted child. The need for a child's ticket was tied directly to the child's age. If under two years of age, we would be allowed to carry her on our lap and not have to purchase a ticket, but if over two, we needed a separate seat. We felt certain the child would be older than two so we purchased the extra tickets.

Next, we had to get passports and final documents from the State Capitol. Once we had gathered everything we needed, we headed to the passport office located inside the courthouse in downtown Tulsa. We found ourselves in a waiting room among others who were also applying for passports. Finally, we went into the small office where we presented our birth certificates, marriage license and driver's licenses to the lady working at the passport desk. We had already filled out the necessary forms and watched as the woman looked over everything. We sat and waited patiently.

She turned to me and asked, "Are you a U.S. Citizen?"

I looked at her, puzzled, and replied, "Yes, of course I am. Why?"

She continued, "Your birth certificate shows you were born in Canada. Do you have your U.S. citizenship documents?"

Bewildered—I didn't understand what she was talking about. She explained my birth certificate was from Newfoundland, Canada, not the United States. I confirmed that I was born in Canada because my parents were in the U.S. Air Force at the time, so I was automatically a U.S. citizen. She told me to check with my parents regarding my citizenship documents. She said I would need to produce the documents before we could proceed and offered to let me use her office phone. I called my dad and explained the situation at the passport office.

"Daddy, do I have U.S. citizenship?" I asked.

"Yes, of course," he replied. "Why?"

"They are telling me I need to prove I am a U.S. citizen. Do I have some kind of documentation showing my citizenship?" I asked.

"Yes, you should have it. I'm sure I gave it to you," he stated, as if I knew this all along.

I continued, "I have no idea what it is or where it is! I don't think I've ever seen it. I didn't even realize I needed a document of U.S. citizenship. Oh my goodness, please tell me you have it, because I'm sure I don't!"

He said, "Ok, I'll have to search for it and let you know if I find it. But I'm sure I gave it to you. Can I call you back?"

Inquiring if it would be alright to wait until my dad checked and called back, the agent nodded and gave me her direct number.

It was shocking to find out that I had dual citizenship until I was eighteen years old! When I turned eighteen, my parents applied for my U.S. citizenship. And for over twenty years, I never knew anything about it. I thought all along I was a U.S. citizen because my parents were in the Air Force. How could I not be a citizen? And why am I just now learning about this? Would I have even known about it if we weren't trying to adopt a child?

My dad called back and said he'd found it. He had not given it to me after all. So we left the passport office and drove to my parents' home. When we arrived, I asked my dad why I didn't know about the citizenship issue. He explained how military children born outside the United States are registered as citizens of the country where they are born. Every country has different laws, but Canada allowed dual citizenship until age eighteen. At that age, you must declare citizenship in one country. My dad thought he'd given me those papers a long time ago. I was just happy he found them! Now we could go back and get our passports.

Finding out about my dual citizenship would actually become important information for us when we adopted our daughter from Ukraine. I would later learn that she would have the same arrangement as I had and would have to declare one country of citizenship by the age of eighteen. *Funny how God works.*

Charlie and I didn't have a Last Will and Testament, but decided now was a good time to make one just in case something were to happen during this trip. We bought a Will Kit and filled everything in, making sure our young son and possibly, newly adopted daughter were provided for, if the worst happened. With our will complete, we were ready to go.

# CHAPTER 12

# Destination: Ukraine

## Tuesday, November 9, 1999

**DAY 1**

The final instructions for our trip to Ukraine included a list of items to take with us, the most important being the amount of cash needed. We were told to hide cash on our bodies and the cash must be brand new bills or at a minimum, very clean bills. At our bank, we explained this to the bank manager. I would use a money belt strapped around my waist and Charlie intended to use a strap around his ankle that would be hidden inside his boots. I felt like we were doing something illegal. Strapping $14,000 on our bodies was a lot of money!

Maren told us to dress casually, in neutral colors, and not to wear anything that would draw attention from others. *Weird.* While packing for the trip, I pondered those instructions and

worried about Charlie's snakeskin boots. *Don't draw attention?*
*Uh, those definitely will!* I shared my concern with him. Charlie
said he felt most comfortable in those boots. He only had work
shoes which were actually tennis shoes and one pair of dress
shoes which he said were definitely not comfortable. He insisted
on wearing his boots. The instructions said NO tennis shoes or
jeans! Definitely too American. We can't even dress normal. *Lord,*
*what are you getting us into?*

All these instructions made me feel uneasy. Why all the
secrecy? People of Ukraine are very proud, Dillon informed us,
and did not appreciate Americans coming there to "take away"
**their** children. Thus, we didn't want to give them any reason to
think we were Americans. We were told we needed to blend in.
*Wow! How do I **not** look American? Are Ukrainians that much dif-*
*ferent?* Why are we just now finding out about all of this? Did
Dillon think it would scare us off if we were informed sooner?

Finally, we were ready to leave. Charlie said he felt like he
was jumping off a cliff. He had only been on an airplane once in
his life and that was shortly after we were married. My grandmother had died and we had flown to Minnesota for the funeral.
Just the opposite was true for me. I couldn't tell you how many
flights I had been on in my life. More than fifty, for sure, and all
over the world. So flying was not a big deal for me.

Charlie had grown up in Oklahoma, moving from home
to home. He was a true country boy at heart and never cared
much about traveling. On the other hand, I had been many places
throughout my life. Moving from state to state and other parts
of the world had prepared me more for what may lie ahead. Yes,
I was nervous, but also excited about this new journey. Charlie,

even though he tried not to show it, was very apprehensive about what we would face in a foreign country. What was God going to do? I turned all my concerns over to God, knowing deep in my heart He was with us, taking care of us. He was not going to allow anything bad happen to us. I can't explain how I knew, but faith was a big part of it.

We packed all the items Dillon had suggested we take with us. Gifts for our hosts and coordinator, as well as school supplies, articles of clothing, and children's medicine for the orphanage were included. Charlie and I stuffed $14,000 in cash into our money belts. Hiding that much money on our persons seemed devious and somehow wrong, but Dillon assured us it wasn't illegal. Besides clothing and gifts, we packed a video camera, a couple of disposable cameras, a small coffee maker, and a special electrical plug converter I had borrowed from another post-adoption couple we'd met. Purchasing a small Russian language dictionary to communicate with our hosts seemed important to have when no interpreter was available.

The thought of meeting new people and seeing a new country felt like an adventure. I was glad Charlie was with me and anxious to see how he would react to everything! What would we see? Where would we go? We must bring back souvenirs! We ARE actually doing this!

We boarded the first plane in Tulsa on Monday just before noon and flew to Atlanta before heading to Europe. We changed to a much smaller plane in Paris, France. I thought maybe we might catch a glimpse of the Eiffel Tower, but never did. I enjoyed hearing the different languages spoken by other travelers. The last leg of our nearly twenty hour trip took us to Kiev, the capitol of Ukraine.

Our plane landed in Kiev in the late afternoon on Tuesday, November 9th. The time difference between Tulsa and Kiev is seven hours, yet it took twenty hours to get there! We left on Monday and arrived on Tuesday. I knew the time change was going to be a challenge. Charlie and I were happy to be at our destination even though we were exhausted.

The pilot taxied and finally pulled up alongside a couple other planes. We disembarked and waited outside on the tarmac for our luggage to be unloaded and delivered to us. We walked about a quarter of a mile to the terminal. I absorbed the surroundings of the small airport. *Wasn't this the capitol city? Why such a small airport?*

Gray clouds littered the sky and a thin layer of snow covered the ground, piling up along the outer fence line. Light snow fell as we slowly moved along with the other passengers toward the terminal. The cold air didn't feel the same as Oklahoma winters where humidity affects the highs and lows much more. My light coat would be just right. I smiled. *Thank you Lord for a safe arrival.*

Somehow we managed to lug our heavy suitcases up an outside set of stairs to enter the terminal. The interior of the airport terminal reminded me of our Tulsa airport, but even smaller. *Again, isn't this the capitol?* At least there weren't a lot of people, which was a relief. I looked around, while keeping up with our fellow passengers to see where they were headed, trusting they would lead us in the right direction. We ended up in a line waiting in front of a row of what looked like check-in booths that blocked us from further entrance into the broader terminal. When we reached the front of the line, we handed our passports to the man seated behind the window in the booth. He spoke English as he handed our passports back, then showed us a form, indicating we needed to purchase medical insurance for our stay in Ukraine. Seemed like an odd requirement. Surprisingly, it only cost $10 per person. *Only $10? What's that going to cover?*

We paid for the insurance and moved to another line where we presented our passports again. The sign above the booth read: NO UKRAINIAN VISA. The gentleman seated in the booth looked up and asked where we had arrived from. We told him we were Americans and had arrived from Paris, France; NOT from the U.S., just as Barbara had instructed us to respond. I don't know why Barbara had instructed us to say that; we never asked for explanation. Maybe it would have meant we would have to go through a different process but I really never knew why. Regardless, our passports were stamped and handed back. So far, so good.

Following the other passengers, we soon found ourselves standing in a long winding line of at least fifty people waiting to pass through CUSTOMS. A young man came through the line, handing us a "Declarations" form to fill out while we waited in line. The form (printed in several languages) required us to list everything we had in our luggage and the value of each item. I was busy reading the form and filling in answers, hearing foreign languages being spoken by others around us when it struck me, we might be the only Americans here.

I looked up as we neared the end of the line and saw two signs posted above separate doors. One read: DECLARATIONS

OVER $400, the other: DECLARATIONS BELOW $400. I didn't know if that meant cash to declare or value of items. Remember, we had $14,000 in cash strapped to our bodies which we weren't declaring! Quickly, I did some mental math of the items values on the declarations form; below $400. Not counting the money belts. I had to remind myself again; this is what Barbara told us. Everything will be ok. *God, you sent us here. I know you will take care of us. Be strong.*

After an hour, we finally reached the last step where an inspection had to be made of everything in our luggage. We hoisted our suitcases up onto a metal table. Charlie and I patiently watched as a female customs agent opened our bags, rummaging through the items we had brought as gifts. I was a little nervous. No, I was extremely nervous. What was she looking for? Was she going to send us to a room where Ukrainian security drills us? What if they discover the hidden cash we hadn't declared? *Hey, Barbara, you didn't mention this part.*

The process was intimidating. The agent pulled out several items, asking why we had a video camera, office supplies, candy and children's medicines. *What do I say?* I swallowed, breathed and told her we were in Ukraine to adopt a child and intended to give several of these items to workers in the orphanage. I held my breath. I didn't know what she would say, but I told the truth and I knew God was in control. *Have faith!*

Suddenly a huge smile spread across her face as she said, "Oh, is wonderful what you do here!" Her English was a bit broken, but she continued, "Some little child very lucky. They lucky go to America. Will be much great life there! I happy what you do here!"

*Whew. Relief!!* I'll never forget how her response was like having another weight lifted off my shoulder—another answer of confirmation about what we were doing. *I can hold my head up and walk proudly. Yes, this was God's will! Why was I still doubting?*

We gathered our luggage and exited the Customs room, then walked toward a small crowd of people facing us who were gazing at all the newly arriving passengers, obviously anxious to welcome their relative, friend or other associate. Scanning the crowd, I spotted a young man holding up a small cardboard sign that read: POTTERS. *Ok, here we go.* Approaching him, Charlie said, "We are the Potters." A second young man who appeared to be in his early to mid-twenties, leaned in and shook our hands, introducing himself, in English, as our interpreter, Alex. He introduced the 'sign holder' Viktor, an even younger man, as our driver. Both young men seemed pleasant enough. They grabbed our luggage and led the way outside.

Light snow fell as we walked with our escorts toward two small cars that were parked not far from the doors we had just exited. I looked around at the bleak surroundings. Trees had shed most of their leaves by then, nondescript buildings lined the opposite side of the drive, no signs or street lights and very few vehicles were scattered in the parking lot. Only the light emanating from the airport entrance bled out onto the street. I glanced at my watch (which I had adjusted to the local time zone). It was 6:45 p.m.

Alex placed our luggage inside one of the small sedan's back seat and trunk. *Hmmm, we need two cars just to fit the luggage?* Alex exchanged some words with Viktor, in Russian, as he climbed into the driver's seat of the first car. We climbed into the rear seat of the second car, which was similar to the size of a Toyota Corolla. Charlie's 6'3" frame barely fit in the space as he twisted his knees toward mine. I'm 5'10"—almost as tall as Charlie! To say the least, we were cramped.

Viktor dialed up the heat in the car and sped off, driving way too fast! *Streets are covered with snow and these guys are driving recklessly!* Suddenly, memories of living in Germany where people drove fast with no speed limits, sprang forward in my mind. I wondered if there were no speed limits here, either. The streets had no lane markings. Vehicles zipped in and out and around each other, moving in every direction, creating their own lanes. We couldn't say anything to Viktor. He didn't understand English. My heart's racing. Heater's blasting. *This is crazy! I hope we don't have a long drive.*

I looked out the car windows as they drove us to the host family's residence, trying to commit to memory everything I saw along the way. I was tired, hoping we would have a nice place to stay. The seven hour time difference didn't help as I duly noted; darkness had already descended. I didn't see houses, only large high rise apartment buildings that were difficult to distinguish in the waning light. Since I didn't see individual houses, I assumed we must be going to an apartment. Barbara had not been clear on exactly what type of arrangements had been made. *Well, I guess apartments are ok.* Little did I know how different apartments were in Ukraine compared to what we were used to in America.

Thirty minutes later, we arrived at an apartment complex and stepped outside the car. I was more than anxious to escape the over-heated vehicle and stretch my legs. I looked around at many large multi-storied apartment buildings with no unique characteristics whatsoever. No color, no design, no landscaping, nothing but dull gray block as far as I could see. The complex looked like a prison. We entered on the first floor of one of the multi-level structures and walked down a narrow dark hallway. At the end of the hall was a small, ancient elevator. *Surely we're not going in that! I doubt four people could squeeze in there!* But in we went, luggage too! I held my breath. Slowly the old, rickety elevator ascended and we all poured out on the fourth floor. *Exhale!*

We were greeted by a middle-aged couple who only spoke Russian. Alex interpreted for us as we were welcomed into their tiny apartment and shown to our temporary bedroom. Our luggage was placed in the small, dark paneled entry area of the apartment. Alex told us he would be leaving and to expect our adoption coordinator who would arrive soon to explain everything. *You're leaving us already? With people we just met and who don't speak English?*

Charlie and I said goodbye to Alex and Viktor as we stood awkwardly alongside the Russian couple in the entry. *I hope the coordinator gets here quick!* We hung our coats on some hooks attached to the paneled wall just inside the front door and carried our luggage into the small, dimly-lit bedroom where we found a king-sized bed that nearly filled the space, with just enough room left over to squeeze along each side. Automatically, I brushed my hand along the inside wall for a light switch, but there wasn't one. Only a lamp atop a small bedside table illuminated the tiny bedroom. We noticed a folded up crib leaning against one wall. I suspected the hosts may have used the crib for other adoptive families in the past.

Without having to speak, the host couple managed to show us the apartment by just pointing toward the living room, a second bedroom, the kitchen, and the bathroom, all of which we could get to from the entry area by taking about five steps in any direction. We nodded, exchanged smiles and I said, "Spasibo." I had at least learned how to say 'thank you' in Russian. We ended up in the living room, waiting for our adoption coordinator to arrive.

The living room consisted of an antiquated sofa, a matching chair, a free-standing book shelf, and a small TV sitting on a table in the corner. The floor was covered with worn and wrinkled brown print carpet, the walls with faded, flowered wallpaper; all of which looked like something out of the fifties. I estimated the entire two bedroom apartment was around six hundred square feet (about the size of a three-car garage). I'm sure the couple who lived here were used to the space, making it fit their needs just fine.

Soon, the adoption coordinator arrived. Klara, thirty-five(ish), introduced herself. She held her head high on her petite frame, speaking in a soft, but purposeful voice. Naturally wavy, shoulder-length brown hair fanned out and over the collar of her heavy winter coat and wool neck scarf, both of which she didn't remove. I was pleasantly surprised at how she spoke English with confidence and only had a slight Russian accent. She said she lived across the courtyard in one of the other apartment buildings and was currently working with another American couple who were also adopting a child and would be joining us the next day at the Adoption Center. *Oh good! We'll be with other Americans.*

Klara sat with us in the sparsely furnished living room, coat and scarf still on, pulled some papers from an oversized vinyl satchel and rushed through our agenda. She asked if we brought gifts and money. *I guess we're going to get right to business!*

"Yes," Charlie said, "did you want to see everything now?"

"Yes, please. Go lay it all out on the bed in your room so I can look at everything," she replied. "Hold onto the money until the accountant arrives. He will be here tonight to collect the fees."

She explained that the accountant handles the money and may take some of the other items. We would keep the few remaining gifts and the children's medicines to take to the orphanage. I hoped our gifts were acceptable. She gathered several items she said would be appropriate for the officials we would be working with while going through the adoption process, but didn't say whether our gifts met with her approval. Then she left the apartment. *That was fast!* No time for conversation: "Very nice to meet you." "How was your trip?" "Tell me more about your family." No. None of that. Klara came across as strictly "all business." She was in and out in twenty minutes. I was confused. We both were. It wasn't the first time we'd feel nervous and out of the loop.

We were once again alone with the Russian-speaking hosts. I grabbed the travel-sized Russian dictionary and tried a few phrases which I'm sure I badly botched. Our hosts seemed to enjoy the brief exchange, nodding and smiling at my effort, only correcting a couple of words I'd mispronounced.

It was getting late, but Emma, our modest fifty-something hostess, must have known we hadn't eaten, so she went to the kitchen to prepare a small meal for us. Soon, the aroma coming from the kitchen made me realize how hungry I was. She reappeared, saying, "Yēst" (eat) and motioned for us to come to the kitchen. We entered the quaint little kitchen to see a wooden dining table, not much bigger than a card table, set with benches on two sides, pressed up against the back corner of the room. The small kitchen included a sink and oven on one wall and a tiny table-top refrigerator on the opposite wall. There were a few cabinets over the sink and oven, but no counter space at all. *Surely they had other storage for food and dishes, didn't they?*

The meal she prepared was delicious. We were offered Coca-Cola or bottled water to drink. She left the kitchen while we ate. *Perhaps she and her husband had already eaten.* I wondered why every item she prepared had chives sprinkled all over it. *What's with the chives? Strange.* There were mashed potatoes, bread, and some kind of meat, possibly poultry or perhaps pork or something else I couldn't quite identify. It certainly didn't taste like anything I'd eaten before. After we ate, Emma asked, slowly in Russian, if we wanted coffee or tea. I recognized the words and replied, "Nyet, Spasibo." (No thanks).

A short time later, while we waited in the living room, the accountant showed up. The young man didn't speak English, but we knew what he wanted; our cash. Charlie had an envelope already laid on the bed beside the remaining gifts we'd brought. The accountant took the envelope and nothing else. He looked at us, sternly nodded, turned and left. Fourteen thousand dollars just walked out the door in the hands of a stranger! My stomach lurched and Charlie looked pale. *I sure hope we're doing the right thing!*

• • •

I don't think I could have gone through with any of this if I didn't have complete faith that God was fully in control of everything. Here we were in a strange country, halfway around the world, allowing complete strangers to look through our luggage, take items we'd purchased, and walk out with $14,000 dollars of our hard earned cash. What if this had all been some elaborate scam? What if one member of this operation was dishonest? Imagine! Honestly, it was scary! I had to believe Dillon International had fully vetted these people. I had to trust God and remind myself how He had been in each step of the process.

• • •

Now going on ten o'clock, we were exhausted. We thanked our hosts again and pointed toward the bedroom to let them know we were going to bed. Charlie wanted to take a shower before joining me in the bedroom. When he returned, he said, "You've got to see the bathroom! I've never seen anything like it. There's one faucet over the sink that swings from the sink to the tub. There is no shower. I could barely move in there," he continued, "but the toilet is in a separate room to the left."

I laughed and said, "Yes, I used the toilet while you were in the next room. You're right, I've never seen a toilet where you have to lift a knob on the tank top to flush. The toilet paper is like recycled brown cardboard. I was almost afraid to use it. I'm sure we'll survive. We won't be here very long."

Our hosts had given us their master bedroom and moved to the second, smaller bedroom, for the duration of our stay.

I prayed, *"Thank you, Lord, for bringing us safely to Ukraine and providing nice hosts to stay with. Lord, I'm trusting you. Keep us safe and let 'Shelby' know we are on our way to meet her."*

# CHAPTER 13

# Kiev to Kharkiv by Train

## Wednesday, November 10, 1999

**DAY 2**

Emma, donning a smile, wearing an oversized uniform style dress and apron, served us a wonderful breakfast of pancakes, sausage and fruit. I had never tasted anything quite like it. Delicious! Klara and Alex arrived shortly after breakfast, a little before 8 a.m., to take us to the city. Outside, the wind chill hit us like an icy spray mist off a waterfall. How I wished I'd brought a hat and scarf. Skies were thick gray and overcast. Snow lightly covered the ground. We left the apartment complex and drove for nearly thirty minutes before arriving at the adoption center in Kiev. I peered out the car windows as we sped toward the center of the city. I did not see any houses, only apartment buildings. *Did people own homes?* There wasn't much to see other than tall gray block buildings, unmarked streets, and barren trees. Not even evergreen trees. *Weird.*

Klara was definitely "all business" with her eyes focused straight ahead and no smile. She didn't talk unless necessary. Getting the job done was all she seemed to care about—dedicated entirely to her role as our adoption coordinator, making sure she did everything "by the book." As a result of her "all work-no play" demeanor, I found it difficult to converse with her about anything other than the adoption. *No time for chit-chat with her!*

Alex, however, enjoyed talking! He was very confident and loved sharing everything about himself. I'd later be reminded of Alex when the Harry Potter movie character was hugely popular. He had the same black, round-rim eye glasses and dark hair. Alex was taller though and more of a preppy college student type. He seemed very happy doing this job, chatting and smiling through his own glaring ego. We had a hard time getting a word in. He explained that he'd been a transfer student to New York a few years earlier and been taught how to be an English translator. I enjoyed listening to him speak about himself, his work, his family, and his hopes and dreams. I found his positive energy very inspiring.

We arrived at the adoption center before 9 a.m. Klara parked in the rear of the building and we all walked through a side door entrance. Klara brought a wrapped bundle of roses with her and told us to sit down on a bench positioned along a wall outside some offices. *Why the roses?* I guessed maybe she had a friend there or maybe it was a gift for someone, but not one of our gifts. *Odd.* We waited as she went into one of the offices opposite from us, watching as the door closed behind her. Sitting quietly with Charlie and Alex, I surveyed the surroundings. I noticed an older couple, possibly Americans, sitting on another bench near us. Otherwise, we were alone.

Soon, Klara returned from the office and asked us, along with the other couple, to come inside. We were all introduced to the center's director, a middle-aged woman, who led us to a table in a small room. The older couple sat opposite of us, a little further down. I could hear the man speaking English, so I assumed this was the couple Klara had mentioned the night before. The director left the room for a few minutes, returning with some large black binders. She put one in front of us and another in front of the other couple. Alex and the director sat across from us. She spoke Russian as Alex interpreted, telling us to look through the book that held pages of photos of children available for adoption.

Charlie and I found ourselves looking at the faces of small children, most just babies. Beside each photo was a printed bio with the orphanage they were placed in, but it was all in Russian. I looked up and said, "We want to adopt a girl around three years old." The director, through Alex, told us these were the recommended children available for adoption. She continued to flip the pages showing us photos of boys and girls. Each page showed a small photo of a child that looked like a baby to me. I was confused. It occurred to me, maybe the children didn't look like these photos any longer. Perhaps the photos were old and each of these children would look much different when we actually saw them in person. *That made more sense.*

The director told us there were many more boys available than girls. She said most of the girls were under the age of two. *Whoa! Back up! I thought they had been told we wanted a girl around three years old.* I clearly remembered Barbara telling us there were many girls available for adoption. Could it be the interpreter misunderstood or maybe there were just fewer girls to choose from than Barbara knew? We had only looked at a few photos when Klara spoke with the director and we were told it was time to leave. *But wait! We didn't see all the photos! Strange.* We had only been there about fifteen minutes!

Klara told us she had all the information regarding the orphanage we would go to, where we could see all the children available for adoption. I was surprised she knew which orphanage we were going to after such a short visit at the adoption office. We hadn't shown interest in any particular photo. I asked her how many orphanages were in Ukraine, so she proceeded to tell us about several locations throughout the country. She said she wanted to take us to one of the best, located in Kharkiv, the former capitol of Ukraine.

I felt lost and confused, not knowing everything going on behind the scenes. *It's hard not being in control!* We seemed to be on a "need-to-know" basis. I had more questions than answers. *Did Klara and the agency already have everything planned for us ahead of our arrival?* Our visit to the adoption office didn't seem important at all. It seemed to be just a formality.

Klara explained that the orphanage we would visit was on the east side of Kharkiv, located in northeastern Ukraine, just across the border from Russia. She told us there were several girls there who matched most of our requirements. I found myself very impressed with Klara. She stayed on track and never missed a beat. She was in control and even though I had lots of questions, for some reason, I felt I could trust her. She actually reminded me of myself, a gal in charge. She knew where to go and what to do. *What else could we do but trust her?*

After leaving the adoption center, we squeezed back into Klara's small car. Next stop was a travel agency, not far away. We parked, handed Klara our passports and watched as she went into a small office to collect documents we would need for our travel to Kharkiv. We waited in the car with Alex, who talked and talked. I like to think he really wanted us to know him and his life in this country. Or, perhaps it was just a great time to practice his English! Either way, we began to like Alex more and more.

Peering out the windows of the car, I saw many tall concrete buildings lined up for nearly a block, in what appeared to be a business district. All sorts of people, most of whom were men, walked among the structures along the paved sidewalks, going in and out of various establishments. Lots of people walking. *Where are they all going?* Again, we waited in the car for Klara to return. Alex talk some more.

Collecting the travel documents took about thirty minutes. Klara then drove us downtown to purchase train tickets. She told us to look around while she went to the ticket office. *Yay, let's get out of this car!* We walked around with Alex to see some of the sights neighboring the area.

This appeared to be a very nice part of the city. A variety of small touristy shops lined the streets and touristy people moved along casually, looking at the sights and popping into shops. *Any Americans?*

There was an old orthodox cathedral across the road, surrounded by trees and park benches. With Alex's permission, we went inside. It was historic and stunning! Filling the interior were antiques, statues, and ornate artwork. A warmth washed over me as the sunlight filtered in through the floor-to-ceiling stained glass windows that stretched along the expanse of the interior. *What a beautiful place!*

Upon exiting the cathedral, we noticed a small deli across the street. Alex told us we could go exchange our currency inside the deli. Charlie thought it would be cool to take some Ukrainian money (called grivna) back home to give to Cody. We went inside and made the exchange.

The three of us met up again with Klara after she'd finished at the ticket office. It was close to 1 p.m. when we piled into her car for the return trip to the host family's apartment. She told us to pack enough to last a week in Kharkiv, then said we would be leaving for the train station at 8 p.m. that evening.

Emma prepared lunch for us. More chives on our food. Instead of sprinkling food with salt and pepper like Americans do, apparently they used chives. *Actually, maybe that's healthier.* We ate and then went to the bedroom to take a nap. Adjusting to the time difference was still wearing on us. We hadn't even been in Ukraine one full day and were already worn out.

Taking into account the seven hour time difference between Kiev and Tulsa, we asked to use the host's phone so we could call my parents to give them an update. In preparing for the trip, we had purchased a calling card that allowed us to make phone calls to the U.S. The card had a set limit of minutes for international calls. First, we dialed the number on the card to be connected to an operator. Second, we gave that operator the card I.D. and waited for the operator to verify the available minutes. Then we provided the phone number for my parents and she placed the call. This process alone took several minutes. Finally, my dad answered and I gave him an update. He was happy to hear from me and wished us luck. I told him I would call again once we had more information. Hearing my dad's voice felt reassuring; a brief few moments of connection with home. *Ok, I feel better now. Let's go.*

Shortly before 8 p.m., Alex and Viktor arrived. It was dark, cold, and damp outside the apartment complex as Viktor and Alex carried our luggage to the waiting cars. Charlie and I followed close behind. Emma, our thoughtful hostess, had given us a small paper sack filled with some homemade sweets and bread she had prepared for us to take on our trip to Kharkiv. I really liked her! We didn't have any clue how long the train ride would be or what to expect when we got there.

Off we went to the train station in Kiev. Charlie, Alex, and I were in one car; Viktor was driving a second car with Klara and her husband. This was the first time we'd met Klara's husband and it would be the last time we'd see him. He and Viktor would have to drive each car back home after dropping us at the train station. Only four of us were going to Kharkiv. When we arrived at the station and exited the car, Alex grabbed our suitcases but Klara pulled Charlie and me aside, looking around to make sure she wasn't being overheard. *What's this about?* She spoke softly, "Please stay close to me and don't speak while we are in the train station. Do not make direct eye contact with anyone. You do not want to draw attention. Just stay close." *Ok. Got it. I'm definitely staying close!*

The train station was huge, sprawling in several directions. *I'm anxious.* Each of us hauled a piece of luggage as I grabbed

Charlie's free hand tightly while the four of us moved through the overly crowded train station. It seemed like an eternity as we carefully navigated through the herd. Travelers were moving in and out quickly and pushing us from every side, like a swarm of buzzing honey bees on the hive. *Please don't look at Charlie's boots.* I was afraid of getting lost if I took my eyes off Klara who seemed to be gaining ground ahead of us. I turned every few seconds to make sure Alex was keeping up as well. Finally, we reached our destination. *Breathe.* Klara handed a ticket to Charlie and one to me as she turned and stepped up into the train first. She asked the train attendant to show us to our cabin. We didn't dare speak. Klara and Alex were staying in another cabin close by.

We settled in for an overnight ride to Kharkiv, Ukraine. Our tiny cabin consisted of two stacked bunks on one side, a narrow sitting bench with a cushion on the opposite side, and a fold-out metal table in the middle, underneath a window. Below the table was a wall heater blasting hot air into the cramped space. We could barely move around. Charlie remarked, "If this trip doesn't kill us, the heat in here will!" Controls for the heater were nowhere to be found and soon we were actually sweating! *How do people handle this?* I asked Charlie if one of us should go find Alex's cabin. He decided to go. Alex asked the train attendant how to turn down the heat, who said there weren't any controls. *Oh my!* We even tried to open the window, but it wouldn't budge. Charlie soon said he was feeling nauseous, but what could we do? Nothing. *We'll just have to suffer through it.*

I tried not to dwell on the heat or the cramped space. Instead, focused on seeing whatever I could looking out the window. Listening to the steady clickety-clack of the train moving along the tracks toward Kharkiv reminded me of a similar train ride I took with my parents and sisters while living in Germany. My dad took us to visit the Berlin wall. I was only 14, but that train ride still haunts me to this day. We crossed from West Germany to occupied East Germany in the dead of night. At one stop along the way, I watched out the window as Soviet guards looked through the passports of all on board. I didn't fully understand how serious it was until much later when my dad explained it all to me. Now I'm travelling with my husband to a former Soviet occupied city but on a completely different mission. *Lord, you were with me then and you're with me now.*

My mind bounced back to the present. Still peering out the window, the moon was hidden behind cloud cover which made it difficult to see much of anything. Once in a while some street lights shone in the distance or faint light escaped from structures, allowing the surrounding landscape to appear for brief moments at a time. The barren earth was still covered in snow with a few trees dotting the landscape. I could make out outlines of small farms or maybe they were old buildings of some kind. It was too dark to be sure. I did not see any vehicles. We were in the middle of nowhere heading toward the far eastern edge of Ukraine. Exhausted, Charlie and I were finally able to get a few hours of sleep.

# CHAPTER 14

# Arrival: Kharkiv

## Thursday, November 11, 1999

**DAY 3**

We arrived in Kharkiv at 7 a.m., nearly nine hours after leaving Kiev. *What a relief to finally be off that train!* Alex and Charlie collected the luggage and the four of us walked toward the front of the station where we were met by a new interpreter, Pavlov, and our new driver, Maxim. Both men were average height and build, with dark hair and brown eyes, not unlike most of the men we had seen so far. *Haven't seen anyone with blonde hair or red hair.....strange.* Maxim and Pavlov appeared to be in their early forties, donned black leather jackets that had clearly been worn for years and smelled of cigarette smoke and sweat. *Oh my....I'll definitely have to get past that.* Right away, I could tell Pavlov was not nearly as fluent in English as Alex. I could hardly understand him at all. Alex finished the introductions, then told us we would be in good hands and left. *I sure hope so, Alex!*

Klara and Pavlov led us to two waiting vehicles. Our driver, Maxim, like the former one, drove fast along the streets of Kharkiv. There were no street markings like we have in the U.S. In Ukraine, apparently drivers created their own lanes. *Are we on a raceway?* The faster they drove, the more likely they were to command the road. If other drivers tried to squeeze their vehicle in front of ours, Maxim would reach down and push a horn button below the dash. As if in reply, other drivers responded by blaring their horns: "I'm in charge!" "No, I'm in charge. I got here first!" "Hey, buddy, move over. I'm coming through!" At least eight cars raced to a screeching halt at a stop light, anticipating the turn to green, like all the horses ready to race out of the gate when the gun is fired! I think I could have reached out my window and touched the next car, they were so close. *This is insane!* I leaned over to Charlie and said, "Well, the heat on the train didn't kill us, but the drivers on these streets might!"

Fifteen minutes later, we pulled up to a large, concrete apartment building where we would reside during our stay in Kharkiv. Just outside the entrance to the building were several large dumpsters overflowing with trash. *Ugh.* Walking past them, we entered the building, carrying our luggage. The apartment was on the third floor. I looked around as we ascended the wide steps. One floor, then another. There were no elevators in this building. Everything was dirty, dull concrete. We maneuvered around empty containers and trash laying on the stair steps as we climbed. There was no color or décor whatsoever, only a row of beat-up metal mailboxes mounted crudely on the wall at the bottom of the stairwell.

On the third level, we walked a short distance to the apartment we would call "home" for the next part of our journey. Maxim ushered us inside, stating this was his family's apartment. He introduced us to his wife, Yana, informing us that they, along with his two young children, would be staying across the hall with his wife's parents. *Wow! What a selfless thing to do. Actually give us your apartment! And add four members of your family to your in-laws' apartment?* He further explained that he and his wife would bring us a meal each morning and evening. *What about lunch?* Soon they left and Pavlov told us Yana would be back with some breakfast. Klara said she herself would take the small children's bedroom and showed us the living room where we would stay. *What? No bed?*

The apartment consisted of an entry area about ten feet square. The kitchen was ten steps from the front door, directly in front of us. What looked like a closet door to the left, near the front door, was actually a tiny bathroom. To the right of the kitchen, still off the entry, was the kids' bedroom. Inside the bedroom were two small beds and some toys scattered around. The living room was to the right of the bedroom that opened off the entry as well. The bedroom and living room each had a door containing full length, frosted glass with a flower pattern etched in them. Standing in the entry area, I could easily see into every room, from left to right: bathroom, kitchen, kids' bedroom, living room. This apartment was even smaller than the one in Kiev. *A family of four lives here?*

Klara showed us a sofa in the living room. This is where we would sleep. *Uh...Ok.* Charlie and I didn't know how we were going to fit on it, but what choice did we have? Didn't it make more sense for us to stay in the kid's room and Klara on the couch? But I wasn't going to say anything. *Was this fold down sofa where the parents slept every night? Wow!*

A telephone on a small table just inside the front door to the apartment caught my attention. Hopefully, we would be able to use it to call our family back home. For now though, we better try to get comfortable. Not sure how long we might be here. *'Shelby,' we are very close now. We'll be meeting you soon!*

I had barely started unpacking when the hostess, Yana, a very young and frail looking girl, came through the front door with some breakfast consisting of bread and fruit. She set the platter on the kitchen table and left without saying a word. She seemed very different from our first hostess. Maybe she wasn't so happy about giving up her apartment while we were there. Perhaps she was just shy.

We went into the little kitchen and sat to eat at a small table set with a red gingham vinyl table cover and red gingham curtains hanging from the kitchen window behind it. The room was so tiny. Only two small wooden stools sat across from each other at the table. *How did a family of four eat in here?* Suddenly, I caught a glimpse of roaches scattering from the adjacent countertop! As I looked around, I saw more near a plate on which a chunk of bread sat. *Ewww! Is that the same bread we're eating? Why didn't the hostess cover it? What could we do?* We had to eat, but Charlie was repulsed and wouldn't eat at all. We had already finished off what Emma had given us while we were on the train. *I guess we're not in Kiev anymore.*

Thirty minutes later, Pavlov showed up and we all left to go into the city of Kharkiv. The adoption office was situated in a business complex among several other non-descript buildings. Klara pulled a bottle of wine out of her bag, handing it to a lady seated inside the front entrance before we entered the office. *Bribery?* Charlie, Klara, and I were led to a room and seated in front of a desk where an unpleasant woman behind the desk began looking through our dossier. She spoke to Klara in Russian and then, through the interpreter, began asking us several questions, more like interrogated us. "Why do you come to Ukraine to adopt a child? How long are you married? Do you have other children? Why not have more of your own children?" Again, I felt as if she had no prior knowledge of us coming. Or perhaps our new interpreter is not getting the message across. *Why was she asking all these questions? Surely, Klara had made an appointment, hadn't she?* I guess we passed the interrogation because Klara suddenly stood up and asked us, "Ready to go?" *You mean we're done? Absolutely! Where to next?*

## CHAPTER 15

# The Orphanage

## Thursday, November 11, 1999

**DAY 3**

K lara briefed us as we drove across the city. She said the orphanage we were going to see was one of the best in Ukraine. It really didn't matter, as I knew God was on this journey with us. He was in control. The drive to the orphanage took about twenty minutes. Along the way, I peered out the car windows at the sights, vehicles, and people. Men and women, young and old, everywhere I looked. The streets were crowded with cars and buses moving in all directions. At a busy intersection, an electric rail car moved down the center of the street, then crossed in front of us. People could be seen walking on every street and sidewalk, carrying what looked like bags of groceries, while others appeared to be business men and women. Some stopped at roadside stands with vendors selling vegetables, fruits, and other items. I had never seen so many people. *This must be the heart of the city.* The two of us wanted to absorb everything in order to one day share this journey with our adopted daughter. Grabbing a camera, I took a few pictures. We only had a couple of disposable cameras, so picture-taking needed to be strategically thought out.

Klara continued to describe the orphanage. She tells us there are no healthy children. *What? No healthy children? Then why are you taking us there?* Then I recalled Barbara telling us we could expect to hear this. Barbara told us that Ukraine does not like Americans adopting their orphans and in order to justify it, they would make up some health condition that could only be treated in America. This would allow Americans to adopt and ultimately take the child to the United States to be "cured." Klara added, "There are very few girls, mostly boys, but you will meet the girls that you saw in the photo albums in Kiev." *But those were babies!*

As we neared the orphanage, I noted the crumbling brick walls that lined the entrance. We drove through the opened gates, pulling up beside a large house trailer that appeared to be the maintenance office. Trees scattered around the exterior of the buildings were still shedding leaves, yet a thin layer of snow lay atop them. A man appeared from the trailer, now coming towards our car. A brief verbal exchange took place with Klara. He then left, returning to the trailer. There was only one other vehicle in the parking lot. *Where were the other cars? Did workers ride a bus to work?* I estimated the entire property to be about an acre in size.

Climbing out of the car, I looked around at several faded yellow brick buildings in partial disrepair and decay. *This is one of the **best** orphanages?* Which building are we going to? There were no signs anywhere. The place looked abandoned. Klara motioned for us to follow her toward a building on the right, up some steps, through a door that opened to a large, partially furnished room on our left. A lady appeared from a hallway at the other end of the room and greeted us. She led us down the narrow hall, into a small office.

An older woman was seated behind a desk in the corner at the far end of the narrow room. Charlie, Klara, and I sat opposite her in chairs set against the wall, a few feet away from the desk. It was tight quarters. Our interpreter sat across from us, next to the desk and interpreted the meeting. The woman behind the desk introduced herself as the orphanage director. She briefly explained the process to us. Some of the children would be brought in so we could look them over. I had to listen carefully to the interpreter as his English was difficult to follow. She asked what gifts we had brought to the orphanage. Klara handed her a bag containing the medicines along with some of the other items we had reserved for the orphanage. She pulled various items from the bag as I watched, curious as to which items she seemed to like. *Why do I always feel like we are "bribing" someone?*

A few minutes later, a female dressed in a pale pink uniform appeared in the doorway, carrying a baby. She held the child up, but she was crying inconsolably while the woman tried to quiet her. The director said something in Russian to the worker that caused her to back out of the doorway. I was confused. I asked our interpreter what was going on. He said the child was not cooperating, so they would bring another. *What are we doing? Trying on fur coats?* The next child was brought into the room. The worker sat down next to the interpreter across from us, holding the little girl on her lap. I looked at this child or what appeared to be about a twelve month old baby and confused, I said, "We don't want a baby! We are looking for a toddler."

The director told us both of these girls were nearly two years old. I was shocked! I looked into the small face of this doll-sized little girl and tried to comprehend what I was seeing. The child was literally the size of one-year-old, a very small one-year-old! The director opened a folder on her desk and began to read from it. She said this little girl (given the name Maryna) was almost twenty-four months old. She was 66 cm tall and weighed 17 pounds. The child had been born in December, 1997, at the maternity home in Kharkiv. She was held there for over a year with no visitors, at which time it was determined that no relative had taken any interest in her. Therefore, she was brought here to be placed for adoption in March, 1999. I listened carefully and thought… *March, 1999, my birthday, my first prayers for Shelby, our family meeting. The timing matched perfectly.*

The petite girl seated across from us tucked her chin in against her chest, her lower lip protruding in defiance, as if to say, *"I'm here, but I don't like it one bit!"* I sensed a shy sweetness sprinkled under that outward display of purposeful defiance. She was definitely small, but adorable with light blonde hair and blue eyes. Just then, Charlie asked if he could hold her. The director nodded and as Charlie reached out for her, she lifted her arms to accept him. With her lower lip puffed outward and furled brow, she appeared to be telling him, "Ok, I'll let you hold me, but I'll be checking you out, too." *Is this her, God? Is it you, 'Shelby?'* Wow! What a powerful moment! The worker let go of her and smiled as Charlie took her into his arms. The director said we could take her out to the other room, spend some time with her and talk with each other privately.

I followed Charlie as he carried the tiny, almost two-year-old girl, out into the hall and then to the larger room which was a good place to have our discussion. Charlie let the child hold his thick calloused finger with her tiny hand, talking quietly to her. The expression on her pouty face with her lower lip protruding outward had not changed. She looked up at both of us, those big blue eyes piercing into our hearts.

Charlie smiled and said, "This is our little girl. Look at these eyes!"

I began to cry, "She's so small, Charlie. I can't believe she's nearly two years old." I touched her cheek and smoothed her thin, white-blonde hair along her forehead. I was still trying to comprehend the fact that she was almost two years old, yet looked like a baby. I continued, "What do you think? Do you think Cody will be ok with such a small child?"

Charlie replied, "We'll have to talk to him and see what he says, but this little girl is so sweet and beautiful. I'm happy and she seems content. I think she's perfect." She sat quietly on his lap without saying a word. I kept looking at her, smiling and watching her expression. *I do believe this is her.*

After only fifteen minutes, we returned to the office, Charlie still holding the small girl in his arms. The director proceeded to tell us more of the child's background. She had been given up at birth by her mother and grandmother. The birth mother was only sixteen years old, so the teen's mother had to give permission on behalf of her daughter. Neither had the means to care for the child and the biological father wasn't in the picture. They felt it best to give up the infant at birth. The maternity home had put in her birth records that she was not healthy and needed expensive medications and possibly heart surgery. The director's next statement was very interesting, "This child has been unadoptable. She has never allowed herself to be held by a man. Every time we had a potential couple come in, she would cry and turn away if the man tried to reach out to her, let alone hold her." She added with a smile, "Mr. Potter, you are the first man she has ever reached out to! We were just remarking on this while you were out with your wife in the other room."

We believed in our hearts this little girl was meant to be ours. We didn't feel there was really anything physically wrong with her. This *was* 'Shelby!' She had let us know by reaching out and accepting us. Charlie and I both told the director that we wanted to adopt and love this precious little girl. The director appeared very pleased as she handed us the adoption paperwork. Charlie gave 'Shelby' back to the orphanage worker. It was time to go. Tears pooled as I turned to look back toward the girl. *We'll be back 'Shelby.'*

The next stop was the notary office in another part of the city, where, once again, Klara gave the notary a gift. *Perhaps the gifts weren't bribes, but just a cultural thing. No, they're definitely bribes—perhaps just to move things along a little faster.* We presented our passports and signed the papers along with the interpreter. Once that was done, we went to another city coordinator's office to drop off the papers. *Why so many places? Why not everything in one location?*

We returned to the apartment to have lunch, which consisted of a light broth with a few small bits of chicken in it, covered, of course, with chives. *What is it with the chives?* I had a piece of bread, but Charlie wouldn't touch it because of the roaches crawling on it earlier. I didn't care. I knew we had to eat whatever and whenever we could. *God, I know you will take care of us.* I knew it deep in my heart. After lunch, we went back into the small living room to rest a while, but Klara informed us we would be returning to the orphanage around 5:30 p.m. that evening. That didn't leave much time for a nap, so I decided to continue unpacking.

• • •

I was surprised we would be returning to the orphanage that evening. We hadn't had time to unpack yet and were tired. Again, we felt out of the loop. Klara was strictly business. I had questions but I didn't want to stir the pot. We just accepted her role as our coordinator and did as we were told. I felt she was just following an agenda and didn't consider straying from it. I got the sense that she thought she might get in trouble if she didn't stick to the exact path; she had to follow the rules.

• • •

I began unpacking and looked around for an electrical outlet to connect the little power plug converter to my coffee maker. I found one outlet in the corner of the room and just as I was about to plug in the special adapter, I was suddenly overcome with the need to document everything we were going through on this trip. I dropped the adapter and turned around. *Do I have any paper?* My focus now was on total recall. I *had* to write it all down. I realized I didn't have any note paper. *Darn, why hadn't I thought of this before we left?* I asked Charlie if he had brought any note pads or paper of any kind.

Charlie smiled and said, "I'll remember it all, don't worry about it."

I shook my head, replying "No, I have to document it! I just don't have any paper!" I frantically dug through my purse until I found some old pay stubs. Don't know why I had those in my purse, but I pulled out three pay stubs along with a pen. I sat on the floor beside the couch, flipped to the blank side of the stub and began to write down everything that had transpired since we'd arrived. I didn't have much space to write in, so I wrote as small as I could, knowing I'd likely use every square inch of paper before this trip was over.

We returned to the orphanage at 5:30 p.m. This time, we were taken to another building across from the main office. As we entered and walked down a long hallway, I listened for the sounds of children's voices, but heard none. We passed one open door where I peeked inside and still didn't see or hear any children. *Odd.* Where were the children? At the end of the hall, we turned and went up a set of stairs. We were in a small open area outside another closed door. Soon, a woman appeared from behind the door, dressed in a faded white, button-up uniform. A brief exchange took place with Klara in Russian. The woman retreated into the room behind the door and soon reappeared carrying 'Shelby'. Smiles all around. Charlie again took the tiny girl into his arms and started talking to her. We found a couple of chairs in the small space outside the room where we could sit down. Klara and Maxim said they would return in about an hour. "Wait, where are you going?" I asked. "Are we allowed to look around?" Klara told us we should stay close to this area, so we settled in.

We didn't know if 'Shelby' could talk. She had not yet uttered anything. I decided to speak to her using both her new name and birth name, 'Shelby Maryna', so she would respond to us and feel more comfortable. It seemed to work. I imagined she must be confused hearing us speak English. She'd likely only heard Russian spoken until now. She had on a two piece, pink terrycloth baby romper that obviously had been washed and worn many times. I held her hand and tiny fingers as she looked up at each of us with curiosity, listening to us ramble on in English.

The hour passed quickly. We handed 'Shelby' to the caregiver who carried her through the door, disappearing into the room beyond, closing the door behind her. *Hope we get to see what's behind that door.* Maxim and Klara returned to take us back to the host's apartment. Dinner arrived from our host across the hall, so we ate what appeared to be exactly the same meal we'd had for lunch. The food we were served here was very bland, nothing like the first hosts' offerings, yet we were still grateful.

# CHAPTER 16

# Let's Take a Tour

Friday, November 12, 1999

**DAY 4**

We arrived at the orphanage Friday morning around 10:30 a.m. to visit 'Shelby.' This time they allowed us to stay until noon. I brought the camcorder along, hoping to videotape some of the orphanage and the children residing there. I wished we had thought to bring something to give 'Shelby,' like a toy or doll or even some snacks. *Maybe we can ask our driver to take us shopping soon.*

Today, our interpreter is not with us while we visit the orphanage. As soon as the caregiver brought 'Shelby' to us, we decided to take a walk with her. Charlie set her down on the floor, holding her tiny hand as we entered the long hallway. 'Shelby' had so many layers of clothing on, she could barely walk. She waddled like a penguin, which was cute to watch, but I felt sorry for her.

*Why did they put all those layers of clothing on her? She had to be uncomfortable and hot!* I removed the coat and hat, stuffing them inside my purse.

I turned around, walking backward carrying the camcorder, recording Charlie and 'Shelby' as we moved down the hall, narrating as we proceeded on our first unguided tour of the orphanage. Charlie held 'Shelby's' hand, walking ever so slowly with her, as not to let her fall over. I had to keep turning to see if anyone was entering our path, but saw no one. Her waddling like a penguin made me laugh out loud. It was so hard to keep from laughing as I observed her trying to walk with so much clothing impeding her forward momentum. She almost fell over several times, but Charlie caught her each time, which made me laugh more. It didn't seem to bother her, she just kept moving or should I say, waddling?

The hallway walls were a drab mustard green color, partially wallpapered and set against a dirty, broken tile floor. We passed by a few closed doors, but heard nothing from behind them. *Where were the kids? Why is it so quiet?* As we neared the end of the hall, we decided to keep going. We descended the stairs, proceeding down another wider hallway, then into a breezeway connecting two of the buildings, lined on both sides with large windows. Still no one in sight. Large ceramic planters filled with tall, green, tree-like plants were placed along the side near some windows where we stopped to look outside. I continued to narrate, videotaping everything. Looking out the windows onto the entrance steps of the orphanage, suddenly the doors opened and several caregivers stepped outside with about ten toddlers in tow. "Look, there are some children going outside! Let's go follow them," I said.

Turning around, we hurried over to the entrance. I grabbed the little coat and hat and put them back on 'Shelby'. Charlie pushed the doors open and we let ourselves outside. Charlie picked 'Shelby' up to carry her down the steps, while I followed with the video camera. The group of kids and caregivers had moved ahead a short distance, but some of the little ones had seen us and were curious. I kept the video rolling, focusing on the children ahead. They stared up at me. Looking past them, I noticed one young woman motioning for us to follow. I smiled and said to Charlie, "Come on, let's go."

These children were bigger than 'Shelby', possibly four or five years old. Each one was wrapped in a heavy winter coat, mittens and cap. I wondered where they were going as I hadn't yet seen any outdoor play area. A few of the children broke away from the group, coming closer to us, chatting in Russian, smiling, pointing up at me as I held the camera. "Hello," I said. One little boy stood a few feet in front of me, pointing up at the odd contraption I held in my hand. He said something in Russian. I wished I could understand. Peering into his dark brown eyes, I kept repeating, "Hello, hello, how are you?" Of course, I continued to smile and wave to all of them. We lagged behind a little to allow the leaders to wrangle the stragglers back in.

Soon, we were behind the orphanage, walking along a path that led around the back of the complex. Ahead of us was a middle-aged couple carrying a small child in their arms. They appeared to be another adoptive couple like us. I shut off the video as the couple approached us. We stopped to chat. They were from Minnesota, also in the process of adoption. They said they had been here nearly three weeks. Charlie and I shared our experience with them. They were shocked at how fast our process was going. I looked up, realizing the entourage we'd been following had disappeared around the corner of the building. We wished good luck to the couple and rushed to find the group.

The other children were now way ahead of us, as Charlie was allowing 'Shelby' to "waddle" on her own. I still hadn't seen any play areas at all. *Strange.* We continued around the corner of another building where we did see a small playground with a couple of metal jungle-gyms and a set of swings. All the other children were there, enjoying some play time.

A few kids were moving toward us as we approached. One little boy, I estimated around three years old, walked right up to me, pointing to the camera, saying something (likely Russian which I couldn't understand). I aimed the camera at him, smiling, then laughing as he tried to reach up and touch the lens. Backing up a bit, I said, "Hello." He responded, imitating me, "Hello, hello." I chuckled some more. *So cute.* Suddenly, two other little ones reached up, grabbing my arms and pulling at the camera. Where did they come from? Now, four sets of arms! Five! *Uh oh!* Suddenly, I lost control of the camera and had to shut it off. I held it up high so they couldn't take it from me. I was surrounded by a multitude of toddlers! *Help! Charlie! Where are you?* Looking around, I spotted Charlie and 'Shelby' way ahead of me! They had never stopped walking. I held onto the camera, shuffling my feet forward carefully, finally pulling free from the toddler pack. Heart racing, I quickly distanced myself, then turned back to look at them, safely smiling and waving, "Bye-bye," while they mimicked me. "Bye-bye. Bye-bye." I rushed to catch up to Charlie and 'Shelby.' *Whew, that was close!*

We rounded the final corner of the orphanage where we could see the main entrance on our right. The maintenance trailer was straight in front of us as we turned back toward the steps from where we had departed about an hour earlier. We had come full circle.

It was time to return 'Shelby.' The caregiver took her from us at the door, then motioned for us to follow her. I was happy to get invited inside the mystery room. She sat 'Shelby' down in a small wooden chair. We stood and watched five children (including 'Shelby') seated around a small table on the opposite side of the room, preparing to eat lunch. Each child had a bowl placed in front of them, along with a small drinking cup and a large spoon. The caregiver gave each child a ping pong ball size chunk of bread, just enough to grasp in their hand, then poured what looked like thin oatmeal into each bowl. Next, she poured some milk from a large pitcher into each cup. Tiny faces anxiously anticipated receiving their bowl and their cup. Once the bowl and cup were placed in front of them, they pounced!

Amazed, I watched those tiny bodies feeding themselves with their own big spoon and picking up the cups to drink milk. I couldn't comprehend what I was seeing. Wee little hands grasping huge spoons, one scoop right after the other, as fast as they could manage until their bowls were empty! Like the cafeteria scene out of "Oliver," one set of hands after another, lifted their bowl, hoping for seconds. *"Please, may I have some more?"* But the caregivers shook their heads, *"No, that's all for you."* Each child carefully held onto the small chunk of bread as they were quickly scooped up and away from their seats, placed back into a crib or in the gated area. More sets of little arms shot up in the air, *"Take me!*

*My turn!"* A second set of little bodies were lifted up and dropped into a chair at the table, ready to repeat the process. *Oh my. Is that all they get to eat? We must bring snacks next time!*

While we stood there, one of the caregivers motioned for us to follow her to another room toward the back. *Oh good, we're going to be able to see more!* I turned on the video camera, narrating as we followed her. We entered another room where I was taken aback at what I saw. I immediately shut off the video camera, embarrassed as I looked down and saw small, naked toddlers sitting on pots (yes, stovetop cook pots!). Several toddlers were seated a few feet apart on pots in the middle of the room, while other children were being tended to around the perimeter. Caregivers were dressing some kids and I watched as they stuffed cloth rags into their pants. *Doing their business on pots? And using rags for diapers? No wonder 'Shelby' could barely walk!* I somehow managed to smile toward the caregiver, nodded, turned with Charlie and slowly backed out of the room. We didn't want to intrude on what was clearly supposed to be private. *Didn't they have a bathroom? Don't they have diapers?*

Back in the main room all the caregivers had apparently finished with lunch and kids were either in the back being washed up or being put to bed elsewhere. We walked slowly toward another room off to the left. I was curious. Approaching the open doorway cautiously, as if an armed guard might appear out of nowhere to block entrance, we were startled as we turned to see a lone caregiver off near the other door who glanced at us but gave no reaction. I breathed a sigh of relief and hit record on the video camera.

We entered a long narrow room, adjacent to the main one, which contained ten small cribs lined up side by side. The opposite wall was filled with windows which stood wide open, inviting in a chilling breeze, briskly whipping across the sleeping quarters. I shivered. I could easily see inside several cribs nearby. Three of them contained bundled, tightly cocooned children, each one sound asleep. *I guess by keeping them wrapped up, the cool air must feel good to them.* I shut off the camera as we quietly exited the room. Walking past the caregiver, I smiled at her. She nodded and smiled back. Charlie and I had been "accepted."

Soon Klara and Maxim returned to take us back to the host apartment for our lunch. As we stepped out of the car in front of the apartment building, I turned toward the front entrance, had just begun walking toward the steps, when something out of the corner of my eye caught my attention. I looked over toward the side of the steps near one of the trash dumpsters and saw a small brown animal scurrying around, obviously searching for food. I said to Charlie, "Awww. Look at that little puppy!"

Charlie turned to take a closer look and then grabbed my hand and said, "Uh, that's not a puppy. It's a rat!" My eyes widened and shudders ran down my spine. *What??? Can't be!* I don't remember ever seeing rats that big. Charlie and Klara both laughed. *Really?? A rat??*

After lunch and a nap, we asked Klara if we could make a phone call to our family back home. We had calculated the time difference and felt it was a good time. I placed the call using the calling card we had brought with us. It seemed like forever before the connection was made. My dad answered the phone. It was so good to hear his voice. I gave an update on our progress and described 'Shelby' to him. I asked if Cody was around and soon I heard his voice come on the line. I held the receiver out to allow Charlie to put his ear close so we could both speak to Cody. We told him about this little girl who was so tiny and not quite two years old. We asked him if he thought she was too young. Cody said, "If you like her, then I'll like her." He said he missed us before handing the phone to my mom. I told her how much we'd accomplished thus far and explained that when we had more information, we'd call again. I felt reassured after talking with Cody.

Our evening visit to the orphanage lasted an hour and a half. Upon arrival, we were again allowed into the main room. As we walked closer to the gated area, tiny arms thrust upward toward us, pleading, "Pick me! Here, take me!" A caregiver walked over and grabbed one of the extended arms, pulling the child up over the wood railing, then plopped him into a chair at the small table. Several children were then served their evening meal that looked to me like the same thing they had at the lunchtime meal. We watched. I again observed kids take and hold tightly onto a small chunk of bread; acting as if they were hiding it. I asked Klara why they did this. She asked the caregiver and was told because they had so little to eat, they held onto food so when they got hungry they had something to eat later. Some would even hide the bread in their crib bedding. Tears swelled in my eyes as I remembered the images of the children in Russia.

• • •

There was one particular little blonde haired boy who stood out to us. Each visit, we noticed him. He always had a smile on his face. I asked about him. The caregiver told Klara (who translated to us) that this little boy was the same age as 'Shelby.' He had been found in a trash bag in the hallway of an apartment complex, abandoned at birth. He had barely survived and was eventually placed in the orphanage. She said he was known as 'the survivor' and had become somewhat of a leader among the orphans. The story of this little boy was so touching that Charlie and I actually discussed adopting him as well. But, we knew we couldn't afford it. We would have had to pay another $8000 cash according to Klara. If we could have come up with another $8000, we might have adopted him, too.

• • •

We returned to the apartment around 7:30 p.m. Klara packed a few items before heading to the train station, explaining that she had to go back to Kiev to finish up some paperwork. Charlie and I remained alone in the host apartment. That night, the hostess delivered a little more food for dinner, consisting of a kind of bologna, soft potatoes (covered with chives), and some fruit. I smiled at the slight young woman and said, "Spasibo," hoping she would reciprocate. She kept her head down while heading toward the door but looked up for a brief second in which I did catch a faint timid smile.

While we sat eating, I noted all the differences in foods and condiments. I remarked to Charlie how little they had here. It felt like we were living in the forties or fifties, maybe in a past century—back in another time. This tiny kitchen contained no pantry of staples. No canned goods, cereals or spices. The few shelves above the sink and stove held only a few pots and pans, glassware and plates. The small refrigerator had no freezer section. No ice. The inside was practically empty. They had no washer and dryer. Not much of anything; nothing like what we have in our kitchen.

I stood quietly looking out the kitchen window and cried; not for my lack of comfort, but for the people of this country. I peered out across the high rise apartment complex that stretched as far as I could see, thinking of the hundreds and thousands of other families living this way; these people were surviving from one day to the next. If there was any consolation, it was in knowing that they knew no different. This is just how they lived.

# CHAPTER 17

# Charlie's Sick

## Saturday and Sunday, November 13 and 14, 1999

### DAY 5 AND 6

At ten o'clock Saturday morning, we picked 'Shelby' up from the orphanage so we could take her with us to get her passport photo made at a local drug store. The store resembled a CVS or Walgreens, only much smaller. *Maybe we will have time to look around after we have her photo taken.* I'd hoped to find an article of clothing that would fit 'Shelby.' We followed Klara to the photo center near the rear of the store. When the photographer directed 'Shelby' be placed in a chair, she refused to cooperate. Each time Charlie tried to set her down, she cried and grabbed him. It was clear 'Shelby' already had an attachment to Charlie. Perhaps it was his red hair she was attracted to. After several attempts to get her in the chair, the photographer suggested Charlie sit and hold her.

With 'Shelby' sitting on Charlie's lap, the photographer was finally able to capture a few acceptable images.

Although we had brought an outfit from home for our new adopted daughter, it was a toddler size 3, much too big for 'Shelby.' She needed a 12 month size! We looked for some sort of baby clothing, but only found diapers and t-shirts which we didn't need. I did pick up some crackers and a box of vanilla flavored cookies before we headed back to the orphanage where we returned 'Shelby.' Around noon, we went back to the host apartment. *I guess we'll have to find another store to buy clothing.*

Charlie wasn't feeling well. He complained of stomach pain and wanted to lie down. When our hostess brought lunch, he didn't want to eat. I ate alone, trying to encourage Charlie to eat something, but he refused. Klara had not yet returned from Kiev, which meant we were on our own. I didn't know what to do. *Can't force feed him!* I really believed he just needed something in his stomach, some sustenance. Was he really sick or just being stubborn?

"Please eat something. I need you right now, Charlie. We're supposed to go back to the orphanage tonight! I want us to be together," I pleaded. But he just turned away.

I wandered over to the window and looked out across the parking lot at all the other high rise apartment buildings and gazed up at the gray overcast sky. Silently, I prayed. *Lord, thank you for bringing us this far and for showing us 'Shelby.' You've been in this all the way. I need Charlie to be healthy. Please give him strength and faith right now. I can't do this alone, Lord. Amen.*

Charlie remained at the apartment that evening while Pavlov took me to the orphanage. Pavlov was very concerned about Charlie. He asked me lots of questions but offered no remedy. I got the impression he was more scared than concerned. I tried to reassure him that Charlie would be fine. Honestly, I felt that Charlie was just overwhelmed with this trip, having a hard time adjusting. What if we had actually brought Cody here? No wonder the adoption agency discouraged bringing children along. There's no way Cody would have been able to adjust to this. Why was I able? Could it be because I was raised in a military family? Was it because of all the places I had lived that I was able to adjust to this place? Likely both of those things allowed me to handle the new environment and culture, but mostly I believe it was due to my increased faith. I knew deep in my heart that God was with me. His Holy Spirit lived in me. *I wish I could take from within me and give this strength to Charlie.*

I visited 'Shelby' alone that night. She was happy to see me, especially as I shared some cookies with her. She gobbled them down and wanted more! I'd better be careful not to give her too much all at once. After all, she's not used to eating cookies. We walked around a bit together until it was time to go.

Maxim and Pavlov returned to drive me back to the apartment. During the drive back, Pavlov told me that Sunday was a national election for a new president in Ukraine. He said we would not go anywhere Sunday evening. He explained there may be unrest on the streets due to protests against the possibility of electing a communist running for the highest office in their country. He said this was actually a run-off, so the stakes couldn't be higher. Many Ukrainians did not want this man to win because they wanted their young democracy to continue. Pavlov said if a communist became president, fearing the possibility, he would flee to Australia with his family.

When I returned to the apartment, I found Charlie still sleeping on the sofa bed. I woke him and told him about my visit with 'Shelby' and everything Pavlov had shared with me. "You have to have nutrition," I said. "Please just eat something. God will take care of you," I continued, "I need you with me." But Charlie didn't talk to me. He wouldn't eat. I felt alone. *Lord, why is Charlie sick? Is this part of your plan? How should I pray? What else can I do?*

Later that evening, I could hear shouting from outside in the streets that continued late into the night. Through the third floor apartment windows, I could make out some people in the distance walking in groups with signs held high. I could sympathize with the fear Pavlov spoke of, so I prayed for peace and God's favor for this country.

On Sunday morning, Charlie felt a little better, so I convinced him to go with me to the orphanage. Pavlov stayed with us as we visited from 10 a.m. until shortly before noon. The caregivers all knew by now that 'Shelby' would soon be leaving the orphanage to join a new family in America. There was one particular caregiver who 'Shelby' clearly favored. The woman always smiled and treated 'Shelby' tenderly, talking to her and caring for her. She was the one who motioned for us to come inside, to venture into other rooms, to see the orphans eating lunch. I asked her (through our interpreter) if she would allow me to take some pictures of her with us and 'Shelby.' She did.

It was a beautiful day. The weather was warmer, yet we noticed many people still wearing heavy coats outside. Why?

The temperature inside the building and in the car was hot and stifling. No wonder Charlie was sick! Both of us were sweating. Charlie was only eating crackers and drinking water. He seemed a little better, but the cold outside, the heat inside, and the lack of nutrition were no doubt contributing to his illness.

Pavlov didn't want to go back out Sunday evening. He believed there would be more unrest in the streets during the election chaos. I decided to use the down time to take some photos around the apartment, catch up on my daily note-taking, and look out the living room window at the surroundings. I didn't want to lay down next to Charlie and disturb him. Instead, I sat in a chair in the corner of the room, listening to the sounds filtering in from the streets while Charlie slept.

• • •

*Lord, thank you for everything you're doing for us. I know you're in control and I trust you to continue to take care of us. Right now, Lord, I'm feeling down and I need your reassurance. My heart is breaking for all these people we've met and seen here, Lord. I've never cried so much. Give me strength to get through this and bring Charlie back to me. I need him and we both need you. Amen.*

# CHAPTER 18

# Paperwork and Ice Cream

## Monday, November 15, 1999

**DAY 7**

Charlie was feeling better when Klara returned from Kiev on Monday morning. She came directly to the apartment to give us an update. All the paperwork had been filed at the capital and everything was right on track. She explained our itinerary for the day. We had a lot to accomplish and I was so grateful that Charlie was back with me! *Thank you, Lord!*

First, we went to a notary office at 9 a.m. We signed lots of papers that had to be notarized and copied. The process for the notary was completely different than in America. Everything was done by hand, taking much longer to complete. No stamps of approval. I looked around the notary office and saw nothing new or modern. There were manual typewriters and an old copy machine; it was the only automated machine I saw. I felt like we were living in the 40's or 50's. Technology had not yet arrived here. Eventually, Klara finished and we were off again.

In November, the grounds and trees were brown and barren but the park areas were kept nice and inviting. I enjoyed looking out the car windows along the way at all the historical monuments on public grounds, snapping photos, and wondered what they each represented. It made me want to learn more about this country and its history. I wish we could have stopped and looked at the monuments but we didn't have time to do that. We just had to enjoy them from a distance.

Soon we arrived at another municipal building in the center of Kharkiv. Klara asked us to wait in the car while she went into the judge's office. I didn't ask why we needed to stay in the car because she made it abundantly clear she had everything under control. *Yes, ma'am! We shall do as you command.*

We waited in the car for at least thirty minutes. I asked Pavlov about the monuments we'd seen. He shared with us that many of those statues had been placed there by Russia prior to the fall of the Soviet Union when Ukraine had been under Soviet rule. He said people living here were not happy with those monuments remaining in their city and hated what they represented. He said several statues were that of the former Soviet leader, Joseph Stalin, ruler of the Communist Party. I understood now why the people of Ukraine were struggling to find their own identity; they wanted to be free from Communist rule.

Klara returned and we were off, yet again, to another office not far away. This time we all went into the building and Klara asked us to wait in a large room where we could sit down. She disappeared with her briefcase of paperwork along with a bag of gifts, including chocolates and champagne. She'd informed us that this was the final and most important part of the paperwork gathering process. We would receive 'Shelby's' original birth certificate and passport. When she returned, she smiled and told us all the legalities were now complete. The only thing left was to have everything translated into English and copies made which she said she'd take care of herself.

We returned to the apartment for a late afternoon lunch, consisting of a few pieces of meat and potatoes floating in a clear broth with chives, served with bread (that Charlie wouldn't touch). It wasn't much, but at least Charlie was eating something. I ate it all and was still hungry.

After a brief rest, it was time to go back to the orphanage to visit 'Shelby'. Klara drove in a separate car, bringing several gifts with her. These included champagne and chocolates that she handed out to workers and caregivers in the orphanage. We visited with 'Shelby' for a short time. I sensed we were very close to the end of this journey. Klara waved goodbye as she drove away while we joined our driver and interpreter who told us they were taking us shopping. *Yay! Finally we get to go shopping.*

As night descended, snow began to fall. The air was cold, winds chilly. We drove to a new part of the city we had not seen before and Maxim asked if we needed to exchange any currency. Charlie and I agreed that we should. Charlie handed a hundred dollar bill to Maxim, but he immediately handed it back, saying it was way too much. Charlie smiled, then showed him a twenty. Maxim agreed with the amount, then left the rest of us in the car while he went to get the money exchanged. When he returned, he gave us the currency and drove to a shopping area. He parked at a corner and all four of us climbed out of the car. Later, I thought about how Maxim could have easily taken the hundred dollar bill and kept some of the exchanged money. We would have never known the difference. Instead, he showed us he was an honest man with integrity.

Snow was coming down heavier now as we made our way around the corner to enter a store. I brushed the snow from my shoulders and looked up to see a very exclusive, two level children's store filled with everything anyone could want for a child. *Yes, this is what I wanted!* As if on cue, a strikingly handsome young man dressed in a suit and tie, approached us and asked what he could help us find. *Whoa! This is definitely a nice place!* Pavlov interpreted while we asked the young man to show us coats and clothing for a young toddler.

"A girl or boy?" the young man asked (in Russian).

"A two-year old girl," I replied. He nodded, turned and led us upstairs, pointing to the outerwear and clothing sections. Charlie and I thanked him, then searched for items to buy for our little 'Shelby'. I was quite pleased Maxim and Pavlov had brought us here.

Surprisingly, the store was practically empty. There were only a couple of other shoppers in the entire place. *I bet a store like this would do quite well in the United States.* The young man hovered close by, patiently waiting to see if we needed anything else; he was ready at a moment's notice to assist. As I began to gather a few items, he motioned with extended arms to allow him to hold them for me. *Wow! Impressive!*

We made our selections, then went back down the stairs to the registers to pay for a two piece outfit, socks, underwear, and a cute little hooded red jacket. Oh, and a sweet blonde haired doll that looked very much like 'Shelby!' Another store employee pointed to a couple displays, asking if we might need any other items. I shook my head, smiled, and completed the transaction.

"Would you like a bag for these?" the clerk asked.

"Yes, of course." I said. The bag was another fifteen cents! *Weird.* This equated to a grand total of about $8.00! *Could that be right?* I'm sure we would have paid at least five times that amount in the U.S. *Hmmm....makes you wonder....*

As we left the children's store, I asked Pavlov what other shops were on this street. He said we could check them out, so we continued along the sidewalk, peering inside the shop windows as we passed by. I was curious about one store front that appeared to have multiple types of foods being sold inside.

"Can we go in here?" I asked Pavlov.

"Yes, but it is very expensive here," he replied. *Curious.... what did he mean by 'very expensive?' Now I **really** want to go in!*

We made our way inside and observed several separate, small kiosks displaying various food items, somewhat like a modern day food court at the mall, but on a smaller scale. Several people were congregating around the food counters, speaking in Russian amongst themselves. The space was not well lit, so we had to walk up closer to see what each booth was selling. Among other things, there were specialty meats, crackers, boxed chocolates, and pastries. Suddenly we spied a counter holding containers of ice cream. "Hey, Charlie, let's get some ice cream!" I said with a big smile.

While I peered down through the glass separating us from the ice cream, Charlie turned to Pavlov and asked him what kind of ice cream he liked. Pavlov reacted shyly, saying, "Oh no, not for me. Cost is too much!" Charlie laughed and told him he wanted to buy ice cream for him and Maxim to take to their families. For us, the price of the ice cream was reasonable and we wanted to share some with our hosts. Once Pavlov and Maxim realized Charlie was serious, they behaved like kids in a candy store! They both scrutinized the ice cream bins and discussed the kind they wanted. They were each so excited, but they took forever to decide! You'd think they never had ice cream before! *Surely they had, hadn't they? At least once or twice in the past? They must have!*

Finally, with ice cream in hand, we continued to look at the other food counters and bought more cookies and snacks from another vendor. We left the shops and headed back outside. Snow was still falling as we walked back to the car. Smiles all around.

That evening, we enjoyed ice cream along with our hosts across the hall. Maxim had taken his ice cream back to his family to enjoy with them, thanking us profusely. Charlie and I remarked to each other how it felt so good to be able to give such a small gift to our hosts and see how happy they were. I couldn't believe how such a simple thing as ice cream brought them so much joy! *I cried.*

CHAPTER 19

# It's Official!

Tuesday, November 16, 1999

**DAY 8**

The final day of our adoption proceedings had arrived! We didn't go to the orphanage that morning. Instead, Klara and Pavlov accompanied us to the courthouse. When we arrived, I asked Klara why there were no signs on the building and how come it looked like a neighborhood apartment complex? She explained the actual court offices were under construction. This building was actually an empty school being used temporarily to house the court. The school was also being renovated at the time.

When we walked inside the building, we were immediately overcome by a harsh chemical odor. There were drop cloths and buckets of paint near the entrance. I covered my mouth and nose and asked Charlie, "Why does that paint have such a strange odor?"

Charlie looked around at a couple of painters and remarked, "They are using lead-based paint." *Ohhhh! That's not good. What if Charlie gets sick again? I sure hope we won't have to be here long!*

So many people crowded into the entry area where we stood, while more were moving up and down the stairs to our left. Painters dripping brushes and rollers moving on walls. No chairs or benches to sit on. *Did anyone think this through?* Klara told us to stay put as she ascended the flight of stairs and disappeared. *Good thing we have her on our case!* I grasped Charlie's hand and closed my eyes. The paint fumes were already giving me a headache.

Soon, Klara returned to lead all of us back upstairs, walking a short distance down a narrow hall where we stood waiting again outside the door to the "courtroom." Klara held a folder of paperwork which I assumed was our adoption file. Finally it was our turn to go into the room. We were told to sit in chairs set along the wall as Klara handed the judge the folder. We sat quietly as the middle-aged female judge, seated behind a school desk at the front of the room, looked through the documents. Soon, she looked up and asked each of us our names and wanted to know which of us would step forward to represent our case. *Strange she didn't ask both of us to stand up.* I looked at Charlie as he said, "Go ahead."

I stood up and moved toward the make-shift bench, facing the judge. Pavlov stood beside me to interpret. Another woman, the inspector, stood beside the judge. The judge proceeded to read from the paperwork a brief description of what was transpiring. She asked me several questions. First, what type of work did Charlie and I do in America? I answered. Second, how would we provide for the child's special needs? I took pause and asked what she was referring to. She said the child had been diagnosed with heart problems and would need emergency surgery. She looked at me, hesitated, then asked if we were sure we still wanted to adopt her. "Oh, yes, we have a wonderful family doctor and medical coverage to take care of any needs our adopted daughter may have," I replied, suddenly remembering Barbara's warning. The judge remarked how lucky this child was to have access to the best medical care in America as Ukraine could not provide it for her. "Yes, ma'am," I said. I felt sure 'Shelby' didn't have a heart problem, but we would definitely have her checked thoroughly as soon we returned home.

The judge asked, "Why do you want to adopt a child from Ukraine instead of having another biological child of your own?"

Knowing God had sent us on this journey, I replied, "My husband and I believe God brought us here. We believe He wants to give this child the best chance at a healthy life and provide her with a loving family and home."

Then the judge asked an odd question. She said, "Do you want to change the child's birth date? You are allowed to move it back as far as six months."

I must have looked confused when I replied, "Why would we want to do that?"

She explained, "Due to the lack of nutrition in the orphanage, the child may be delayed in growth and by moving her birth date back, it would allow her to be closer to her peers on the growth charts in America."

I looked at Charlie and asked what he thought. He and I both felt it would be dishonest to change her birth date and agreed to keep her actual date of birth as is.

At that, the judge smiled and thanked us. She reminded us again of the urgency for a much needed heart surgery. I nodded and said, "Yes, ma'am. We will take good care of her. Thank you so much."

We were directed out of the room and waited in the hall for another fifteen minutes while the judge made her decision. Another man and woman were standing near us in the corridor, speaking English. The man introduced himself and asked if we were there for an adoption.

Charlie smiled and said, "Yes, are you?"

The man continued, "Yes, we've been here almost six weeks."

"Really? We've only been here about ten days," Charlie replied. The conversation continued briefly until we were interrupted by the court inspector who opened the door and handed a folder to Klara. She opened it, read the words and declared, "You're approved!" *Wow! We've adopted a little girl.* It was official. 'Shelby' (now officially Shelby Maryna Potter) was ours.

We wished the other American couple luck as we maneuvered our way around others in the hall, descended the stairway, and finally made it back outside. I was so happy to get away from the paint odor and breathe fresh air again. Klara said she had to make copies and translations of everything. She and Pavlov took us back to the apartment where we were told to start packing. Soon we would be going to the orphanage for the last time.

Charlie and I wanted to call home and let everyone know the good news. My mom answered the phone, so I gave her an update on everything that had happened at the court with the judge. She was happy for us. I asked her to please call our family doctor and make an appointment for us to take Shelby in as soon as we returned. She asked for Shelby's birthdate so she could provide the doctor with that information. Charlie and I felt we would be back home in about a week's time, so my mom said she would let the doctor know. I finished by telling her we would be returning to Kiev that day and would try to call and give her our itinerary before leaving Ukraine.

The host family brought us some lunch, thanked us and said their goodbyes in broken English. We thanked them, too. Klara returned and we towed all our luggage to the car. Let's go get Shelby!

At four o'clock in the afternoon, we arrived for the final time to the orphanage. Klara handed us roses and gifts to hand out to the caregivers. She gave more of our original donations to the supervisor, who was very pleased with the medicines and underwear we had brought from America.

All the caregivers, along with Maxim, Pavlov and Klara, posed for final pictures with us and Shelby. We changed Shelby out of the worn terrycloth two-piece into one of the new outfits we had bought, which she fit into perfectly, then put the new red coat on her and walked out the doors of the orphanage for the last time. She never made a peep. Charlie carried Shelby down the steps as I paused, looked up toward the windows where Shelby had resided for the past year and saw the one lady to whom Shelby had shown affection. She stood there at the window, looking down at me, one hand wiping tears from her eyes, the other waving goodbye. *I wish I'd learned her name.*

By the time we arrived at the train station, night had fallen. I cried when we said goodbye to Pavlov and Maxim. We had learned so much about these young fathers over the past week and felt a bond with them. I dreaded the train ride back to Kiev, but this time was different. We had a slightly larger cabin and also had Shelby with us. She was sound asleep when Charlie placed her gently on the narrow bunk. We both sat on the edge of the bed and prayed for her. She slept through the night.

. . .

We were in Kharkiv for only six days; less time than most people spend vacationing. Yet those six days changed our lives forever! Here we were half-way around the world in a foreign country, living with people we didn't know, had never met, and who spoke Russian! If someone had told us a year ago that next November we would be in Ukraine adopting a child, I believe Charlie and I would have thought they were crazy! But here we were. God had orchestrated the whole thing. He placed this child in our care.

*Lord, you are all knowing, all powerful and greatly to be praised! Let us raise this child in You and let us never forget what You have done. Amen*

# CHAPTER 20

# Final Days in Kiev

## November, 17-20

### DAY 9, 10, 11, 12

By the time we returned to the original host apartment in Kiev Wednesday morning,Charlie and I were not only hungry, but drained of energy as well. Our hostess, Emma, had prepared a wonderful array of breakfast foods upon our return. Charlie was ecstatic. He ate. I ate. Shelby ate so much I feared she would throw up. When we decided to cut her off, she cried for more, but she'd had more than enough. *How is she fitting all this food in that tiny little body?*

Klara arrived later with her teenage daughter, Darya, who wanted to meet Shelby. Darya brought a couple toys with her to play with Shelby, who happily engaged with the young brown-eyed teen. We all sat in the tiny living room and watched Shelby play with Klara's daughter. Darya spoke English well, even better than her mother, so I asked her how she'd learned English. She told us all students were taught English in school. At that point, I recalled how teenagers in Germany also studied English as a second language. *That's good to know...and makes me proud.* We enjoyed visiting with Klara and her daughter but were reminded again how tired we were. Klara told us to stay in and get some rest, explaining she needed to go get some final paperwork done. As they were leaving, she stated that Alex and Viktor would pick us up on Thursday morning to take us sight-seeing. *Wonderful!*

Charlie decided to take a nap. I wanted to give Shelby a bath before napping, so I took her into the small bathroom and prepared a bath. However, when I tried to put her into the tub, she began to resist, crying out as if she was scared. This surprised me. *Had she never had a bath? Or maybe just not in a tub?* I tried reassuring her by getting into the tub myself, practically fully clothed, so she could see there was nothing to be afraid of. She still resisted, but I gently spoke to her and splashed water over her a little at a time, until she realized it was safe.

I dried myself off as much as possible, then redressed Shelby before going to the bedroom. I changed clothes after placing Shelby into the small crib that had been set up for her by our hosts and draped my wet clothes over the railings. Charlie was out like a light. I laid down beside him and soon dozed off. We all slept soundly until Emma knocked on the door around 6 p.m. to tell us our dinner was ready.

The three of us slept well again that night. I felt reassured knowing we were in the final stage of our adoption journey. God had been in complete control all the way. I had never doubted or been concerned that anything would go wrong. Strange that I didn't. I just always had a sense of peace about the entire process.

Thursday, we would be able to spend some time with Shelby sightseeing around Kiev. I looked forward to a day without attending to business matters.

• • •

Our original driver, Viktor, and interpreter, Alex, arrived shortly after we had finished breakfast Thursday morning. Klara continued doing all the final paperwork, including preparing our documents to take to the U.S. Embassy on Friday. We were lucky to be able to spend the day sightseeing and shopping in the city.

Snow covered the ground, skies still a mucky gray as a cold breeze surrounded us while we walked around landmarks, cathedrals, and shops in the center of Kiev. I took pictures to add to our journey collection so Shelby could one day look back and know where she came from. We purchased authentic Ukrainian souvenirs to bring back home for Cody, Shelby and my family. Charlie and I took turns carrying Shelby, who never made a sound. With the snow falling, she kept her hooded head down while outside until we entered a store where she could look around. It still felt like we were carrying an infant, light as a feather. We enjoyed seeing the sites and sharing the day with our new adopted daughter. Before we knew it, it was time to return to the apartment.

Friday morning, Klara and Alex took us to the U.S. Embassy to finalize our adoption papers. All of our documents had to be certified, signed, and notarized. They gave us our exit information for Warsaw, Poland. A few other adoptive families were there at the same time. This took nearly two hours, yet Shelby never uttered a sound. Once everything was complete, we were presented a sealed envelope and told not to open it until we were at the Embassy in Warsaw. *Wonder what's so secret about these documents?*

Next, we were taken to a local medical clinic to have Shelby evaluated by a doctor. The place was crowded and not very clean. Many adults, children, and crying infants lined the halls inside the dingy clinic. Some were sitting on benches, but many others stood leaning against walls, waiting. I didn't feel comfortable having a strange doctor look at Shelby, but apparently it was one of the requirements. Ultimately, we would have her evaluated by our own doctor back home. *Why do we have to do it here?* As it turned out, the clinic doctor did a very basic checkup: ears, nose, throat, and temp check. He looked over the medical papers which had been provided to us by the orphanage. We paid only $15 for the checkup. Relieved, we accepted another sealed envelope to deliver to the embassy in Warsaw.

We were now finished with all requirements in Ukraine, ready to leave for Warsaw, Poland. Klara handed us a large binder containing all the original and translated copies of everything that had transpired while we were in Ukraine. It was about eight inches thick and heavy, to say the least.

• • •

It was still snowing Saturday evening so we bundled Shelby and put on our coats as we traveled to a local indoor/outdoor mall. We were happy, watching people shopping and congregating together in what appeared to be a nice, welcoming spot in Kiev. Still, Alex and Viktor were very protective of us, acting like they were our security guards. I guess in a sense, they were. At one point, Charlie was trying to maneuver through a crowd, holding Shelby. He disappeared. I couldn't see him. He had only walked a short distance but Alex quickly rushed forward to find him. Then I lost sight of Alex, too. Soon, Viktor and I caught up just in time to hear Alex asking Charlie (rather harshly) what he was doing, where he was going, and demanding that he stay close. I think it was totally innocent; Charlie didn't realize he had left us behind. Alex admonishing Charlie suddenly made me feel nervous about the crowd. I tried not to speak, recalling the words of warning from Klara at the train station. "Stay close."

Alex had successfully corralled everyone back together, then ushered us into the indoor part of the mall. A sigh of relief ensued as we entered to find a very nice shopping mall made up of a variety of stores. Unlike malls in America though, these stores had no walls separating one from the next. It was strange to one minute be looking at bed linens, then turn around to the next shelves and see kitchenware. *Oh.....I think we're in a new store now.*

Meandering through each shop, we decided to look for items we could purchase to take home. At one shop, we bought a set of toy alphabet blocks for Shelby that had Russian letters and symbols on them. When we went to the counter to pay, the cashier charged us for the plastic bag along with the toy. This was the second time we'd been asked to pay for a bag. I asked Alex why they charged for the bag and he simply said it was customary. *Hmmm...* We continued looking around and found a few other items to purchase for our family.

Charlie and I wanted to buy "thank you" gifts for Alex and Viktor, so we asked them what they would like. As they were contemplating this request, staring at us as if they didn't understand, Charlie told them to go pick something out for themselves. We continued to look around for a gift for Klara and met the men at the checkout counter. I was somewhat taken aback when I saw Viktor had selected a large bottle of Bailey's Irish Cream Liqueur! Alex admonished the driver for choosing such an expensive item, but Charlie said, "If that's what he wants, it's fine." I laughed, but then thought again how they felt Americans were rich people. The liqueur was expensive, even for us! Alex had chosen a box of chocolates. *Yeah, that would have been my choice, too.*

We gathered all our purchases and soon returned to the apartment. After dinner, the accountant came to the apartment with Klara to give us a cash refund, which was unexpected. He explained it was because we had completed our adoption two days early. We were pleased, but decided to give the money to Klara as an extra thank you gift along with the knit scarf we had purchased at the indoor mall, telling her how grateful we were for everything she had done. She was thrilled! She declared, "I am going to buy real coffee!" I smiled and tears filled my eyes. *Real coffee.* Such a small thing to me was such a big thing to her.

Klara gave us a gift as well. It was a book filled with stories and photos of Kiev and she and Alex had written a message inside for Shelby. We hugged and said our 'goodbyes.' As she prepared to leave, she told us we would need to be packed and ready to go to the airport early Sunday morning.

It was late. We were tired. All three of us slept well.

• • •

*Lord, thank you for this precious child you have entrusted to us. Thank you for Klara! Thank you for our host families. I pray for your blessings on every person who we have been blessed to meet while here in Ukraine. I'm so grateful for being an American and want to be better. Help us to be more grateful, to love our new daughter, and teach her about you, Lord. Amen.*

# CHAPTER 21

# Warsaw, Poland

## Sunday and Monday, November 21 and 22

### DAY 13, 14

E arly Sunday morning we were packed and ready to leave. We thanked our hosts and said our goodbyes. I carried Shelby while Charlie assisted with the luggage. Now we would go to the American Embassy in Warsaw, Poland, the Eastern European headquarters for international adoptions, which included the country of Ukraine. All final documents would need to be approved at the U.S. Embassy in Warsaw where we would receive Shelby's visa.

Traveling now entailed carrying Shelby everywhere we went. *We hadn't thought that one through!* It was a challenge trying to handle our luggage and carry her at the same time. Eventually, we did make it onto the plane. Even though we had a separate ticket for Shelby, she wanted to be held. She slept on Charlie's lap for the hour and a half flight to Warsaw.

We took a cab from the airport to the hotel in the city. Snow covered much of the landscape. The buildings and décor lining the streets were ornate and quite stunning! *What a beautiful city! This must be a modernized part of Europe.* I had never been to Warsaw but now wondered about its history. This amazing "city on the hill" reminded me of what Washington D.C. is in America, drawing visitors from around the world.

Close to noon, we arrived at the hotel, a Holiday Inn, which was a stunning, welcoming sight. A sign of Americana. We checked in and were so happy to have a nice hotel room with a king sized bed for Charlie and me and a cot for Shelby. We made ourselves comfortable while Charlie immediately grabbed the room service menu to read what kind of American food was available. We weren't really hungry yet, so we thought this might be a good time to go look around the hotel and see what the in-house restaurant looked like.

Walking around the main floor of the hotel, we found the restaurant. It was very nice but we still wanted to wait until later to decide where we would eat. There was also a nice gift shop we walked through before stopping at the front desk of the hotel to ask where the U.S. Embassy was located. They showed us a map and we discovered it was not very far from the hotel. We felt this was a good time to take a walk outside and locate the embassy so we would know where it was and how long it would take to get there on Monday. Soon we had located it and then returned to the hotel.

Charlie said he wanted to stay in the room and relax. He looked over the room service menu, ultimately ordering pizza. I could tell Charlie felt much better now. The comfort and ammenities of the hotel allowed him to feel more like he was at home. Pizza arrived, hot and delicious. Shelby ate and ate! Again, I was concerned she would throw up. I was amazed at how much she could fit into that little body of hers.

I really wanted to take a long, hot shower! However, I first decided this was a good time to call home and let everyone know how things were going. Calculating the time difference, I hoped my parents would still be home before going to church on Sunday morning. I placed the call and spoke to my dad and then to Cody, who was thrilled to hear from us. The first thing he asked was, "When will you be back?" I told him we should be back by Tuesday, two days before Thanksgiving. "You better be here for Thanksgiving!" he declared.

After the call, I enjoyed my much anticipated hot shower, then decided to try giving Shelby a bath again. *I hope she doesn't cry!* I prepared the bath while talking gently to her—showing her the tub and much to my surprise, she didn't resist this time! She actually liked the bath. *Relief.*

With each of us clean and relaxed, Shelby was able to lay on the cot and take a nap, while Charlie and I looked over the documents we'd received in Kiev. We wanted to make sure we had all the correct paperwork with us for our meeting at the embassy. Once we determined we knew what we needed to take with us, we felt we could unwind. We watched some television but couldn't understand anything being said, so we turned the volume down. I walked over to the window and looked out over the city below.

Snow continued to fall as I scanned the haze for lights dotting the buildings and glistening on the snow-covered streets. The view was quite remarkable. I used the last two frames left on the disposable camera to capture it.

Monday morning we bundled Shelby and headed over to the embassy, arriving shortly before 8 a.m. We hoped to be first in line but were surprised to see a line of people ahead of us, all waiting for the doors to open. Snow from the night before had piled up quite high all around us. While we stood under a metal canopy outside the entrance, suddenly the weight of the snow caused the entire canopy to collapse! I watched it fall, as if in slow motion. I grabbed Charlie's arm, pulling him and Shelby backward as everyone rushed to the sides of the walkway to escape risk of injury. One woman was hurt and an emergency vehicle arrived soon to take her to the hospital. *That was close!*

With the entrance to the embassy now blocked, we were all directed to another entrance along the side of the building. About an hour had passed before we safely entered the building. We were directed to a room where we presented our passports, sealed envelopes, and all of our documents. They read through everything carefully and asked us how long we intended to stay in Warsaw. I responded, "Only one day. We just adopted this little girl in Ukraine and can't wait to return home." The man smiled but said nothing. Finally, they returned all our documents along with our passports and visas. Now we had what we needed to go home.

We left the embassy shortly before noon. We had lunch in the practically empty hotel restaurant, then settled back into our room for the rest of the day. Tomorrow we were going home. I reflected on everything we had been through—all the places we had seen—the orphans—the people—the work God had accomplished.

• • •

God had done it all. He was in control. We didn't ask a lot of questions. We didn't always know what we were doing, where we were going or why we were there. The entire experience felt like we were part a tour group with a trusted guide taking us to various destinations. The guide spoke a foreign language while pointing out all the historical sites. We were part of the group but were actually alone. All the other tourists spoke foreign languages we couldn't understand. We just followed the group, smiled, enjoyed the views, and somehow knew we would be safe. After all, God was our guide.

CHAPTER 22

# Let's Go Home

## Tuesday, November 23
### DAY 15

Tuesday morning we packed up and caught a cab to the airport. When we presented our tickets at check-in, we were horrified to find out they were no longer valid! I stood back a short distance, holding Shelby in my arms, luggage on the floor next to me, while Charlie discussed the ticket situation. They told him Delta Airlines no longer flew into Warsaw. *WHAT??? There must be some misunderstanding. What are we going to do?*

Charlie was just as confused as I was. He said apparently Delta was no longer servicing patrons in or out of Warsaw. *How can this be?* We bought these tickets only eight weeks ago! Charlie was directed to an office on the upper level of the airport. He told me to stay with Shelby and our luggage while he went to resolve the problem.

Sitting down with Shelby on a bench in the middle of the lower level, I watched Charlie ascend a long set of stairs, walk down a long corridor, and disappear into a room on the upper level. This was the first time I actually felt scared. We're in the middle of a foreign land, people passing by speaking foreign languages. I'm alone with a little girl who doesn't understand English or what's going on around her. I don't know what's happening upstairs. Will we be able to get home at all? All sorts of possible outcomes were playing out in my mind. *Lord, please let this all work out so we can go home.*

I waited for what seemed like hours. I walked around with Shelby, trying to keep her entertained, but I also needed to keep an eye on our luggage. Minutes ticked by. My level of anxiety was increasing. *Why is this taking so long? Here we are in a strange airport, a strange city, a strange country with strangers speaking strange languages! This is a nightmare. Please fix this Lord.*

Finally, Charlie reappeared. He'd been given new tickets on another airline. He said he'd been trying to avoid paying change fees for new tickets but finally had to pay the difference. At that point, I didn't care how much it cost or what airline it was. I was exhausted and just wanted to go home. I was so thankful it had worked out in the end. *Thank you, Lord!*

We boarded a jumbo jet. It was the biggest airplane I had ever seen in my life! There were four sections of seating from front to rear and each section had three seats on the outer aisles, with another center row of five seats. We were in the furthest rear section of the plane in the center row. We had a whole five seats to ourselves. *Nice.* This flight would be over 10 hours long! We settled in.

There were not too many passengers in our section of the plane, which was a relief. We turned the center two seats of our row into a makeshift bed for Shelby to lay on, but she wasn't interested in sleeping. Nope. Sleeping was not on her agenda. Luckily, we had lots of cookies to keep her satisfied. However, soon we ran out of cookies. She started to cry. We asked the stewardess for some snacks and juice, but that didn't do the trick either. I held her. Charlie held her. Nothing worked. All I could think of was how other passengers must be looking at us, wishing they didn't have to put up with a crying baby for the duration. I knew exactly how they felt.

Two hours into the flight, Charlie got up, took Shelby by the hand and placed her in the aisle, walking her up and down the aisles to keep her occupied and quiet. The movement seemed to satisfy her. *But he can't do that for the next eight hours!*

As I watched Charlie walk with Shelby, a woman sitting on the outside aisle leaned over and introduced herself in English! Her pleasant motherly demeanor and sweet smile struck me as she spoke up softly. I engaged with her, happy to converse with another American. I apologized for all the crying from Shelby, hoping it wouldn't continue to disrupt her experience on the flight. She told me she was with a group of twenty missionaries returning from Bosnia, all of whom were seated in our section. A few other women turned and humbly smiled, washing away any fear or embarrassment I'd felt. I was among other Christians. *Thank you Lord!*

I explained we were returning after adopting Shelby in Ukraine. The missionary said Shelby's crying would not bother any of them at all and asked if they could help in any way. I visited

with her as she introduced me to a couple of the other missionaries who proceeded to share their recent experiences in Bosnia.
In return, I shared our adoption journey with them. It was such a
blessing to have them on our flight. Just knowing they were there
eliminated all my pent-up anxiety.

For the remainder of the flight, Shelby was anything but
quiet. We were out of snacks and drinks. She wasn't interested
in the doll we'd purchased for her, nor any of the toy trinkets we
had with us. Charlie kept Shelby busy by continuing to walk with
her, which meant neither of them got any rest. Other than that,
the flight was smooth and uneventful. As we crossed the Atlantic,
we gained the hours lost while in Ukraine. Soon, we arrived in
Georgia exhausted, but relieved. "One more flight, Babe, and we'll
be home," Charlie exclaimed. *Yes, then I can breathe.*

The large, sprawling airport in Atlanta was filled with hundreds of arriving passengers when we entered the massive terminal. Again, we had to present our passports, where this time
Shelby's papers were highly scrutinized and ultimately accepted.
An hour later, we were off to our departure gate to catch our flight
to Tulsa, three tickets in hand.

After we found our gate, we had a few extra minutes, so I
called my parents to let them know what time to expect us. My
mom said someone from Dillon had called to ask if they could
have a local news crew meet us at the airport to interview us. I
told her we didn't want any news coverage. We were extremely
tired and didn't feel this was appropriate. *It's not about us.*

The lady at the check-in counter announced that our flight
was overbooked, requesting anyone willing to sell their seat to
please step forward. I saw a few people step up. Then, the doors

opened and we lined up. When we reached our seat assignments, we discovered our seats were not all together. Only one of us would be able to sit with Shelby. I decided to keep her with me while Charlie was seated two rows behind. I'd hoped this would give him a chance to rest a couple of hours, praying Shelby wouldn't cry the whole time!

The plane was full and suddenly a flight attendant appeared next to my row, leaned over, and asked me if someone was seated in the empty seat next to me. I told her it was my daughter's seat. I was holding Shelby at the time. The attendant then said I would need to place her in the seat or give it up. I was confused. "I paid for this seat. It's for my daughter," I said. "We were forced to buy this ticket for her, even though she is under two years old." She walked away, then returned with another airline representative. He told me they needed the seat, so unless I placed my child in the seat, I would need to give it up.

By now, Charlie had walked over to hear what was going on. The two attendants explained again, they needed the seat. Charlie said he would be happy to sell his seat and take the seat next to me while I held Shelby. The attendants left. Someone else showed up to say he was one of the accounting representatives. He told us the airline didn't want any problems, explaining their policy; they do not buy back a seat that is unused. Charlie insisted on a refund for the ticket we purchased before we would give up our seat. "You paid others for surrendering their seats, so what's different here?" Charlie asked. The man shook his head and left again. I felt like we were holding up the flight. All I wanted was to go home. They returned and agreed to the refund. Charlie insisted on it in writing. *Can we please go home now?*

Charlie moved to the seat next to me, sat down, sighed, and whispered, "I'll never complain about anything ever again."

I looked down at little Shelby Maryna resting her head against my chest, thinking of this precious gift God had entrusted to us, smiled, and replied, "Neither will I."

We were all worn out, physically and emotionally. I don't think I'd ever been so tired in my life. The plane rolled away from the gate and taxied down the runway. I listened as the engines thundered, thrusting us forward, then lifted us off the ground. I leaned my head back, looked out the window at the starry night sky falling into darkness as we rose high above the fading sunset. I closed my eyes. Shelby slept peacefully in my arms for the duration of the flight.

We were home.

# CHAPTER 23

# Just Give It Some Time

I t was so nice to finally be home. I was exhausted. *Can't wait to sleep in our own bed and use our own bathroom.* I was exhausted. (Oh sorry, I already said that, didn't I?) Having to readjust to the time difference again made me feel like I had taken a bottle of sleeping medication before running a marathon. Tired or not, we had to turn our attention to our son. Cody was so happy we were back. His excitement spilled over on all of us. He had made a "Welcome Home Shelby, Mom and Dad" banner all by himself and it hung over the entry to our living room. He met his new little sister and wanted to hold her, but Shelby wasn't quite ready to meet anyone else just yet. She was tightly clinging to her daddy.

We thought we would be coming home with a toddler so we had bought a twin bed and had it all prepared for our new arrival; now we realized that it wasn't going to work. We needed a crib. That first night, we placed the twin mattress on the floor and rolled up blankets to place around our daughter so she wouldn't fall off. Charlie and I took turns all night checking on her. She slept just fine. Good thing she did because the next two weeks would turn out to be a whirlwind of events at which she would be the main attraction.

The next day, Wednesday, Charlie had to run to Walmart to buy some clothes for Shelby because every article of clothing we had previously purchased for her was too big. One of our neighbors came by to meet Shelby and as we were talking, I mentioned we needed to get a crib. Turned out she actually had a crib in her attic and offered to lend it to us. That was a blessing!

Thursday was Thanksgiving Day. We spent it with my family at my parent's house. Everyone was excited to meet our little Shelby Maryna, the newest member of the family. Normally, I would have prepared some side dish or made a dessert, but not this year. It didn't matter. There was plenty of food for everyone, especially Shelby. She must have thought she'd died and gone to "Buffet Heaven!" I'd never seen a child eat so much, and again I thought surely she would throw up. I warned my mom to stop feeding her, but you know how moms are. "This little girl needs to put on some weight," she declared. What could I say?

Saturday was the first of four different baby showers over the next seven days. The first was hosted by my longtime friend and former co-worker, Sharon. Lots of gifts, hugs, and cake were shared. Turns out Shelby LOVES cake!

Sunday morning, we were excited to take our new daughter to church. Right after breakfast I realized we still didn't have a dress for her to wear. All the clothes from the baby shower were too big because everyone was under the impression we were coming home with a three year old. I turned to my husband and asked as sincerely as I could, "Charlie, would you mind running to Walmart and get her a dress so she can make her church debut properly?" And of course, he did. I knew he would.

Monday, I had to return to work. I took Shelby with me because all my coworkers wanted to meet her. They had planned a baby shower. Charlie joined me and Shelby for the shower. More clothes (all too big), toys and more cake. She seems to be developing a sweet tooth for cake!

We always went to church on Wednesday night. That night, the church had planned a surprise baby shower right after the service (shower number three). By then, Shelby had figured out all those colorful gift bags contained lots of fun stuff so she had a blast removing the colorful tissue paper and whatever else was in there. Finished with the last bag! Where's the cake? Yummmmmm!

The fourth shower on Friday was a huge surprise, given by an elderly couple who lived across the street from us in our neighborhood. Apparently, several neighbors had found out about our adoption and planned a shower upon our return. Turns out it was also Shelby's birthday. She had a wonderful birthday with lots of gifts, more new clothes, stuffed animals, toys, and yes— MORE CAKE!

Saturday, we celebrated Shelby's birthday with our family. Please don't ask me to tell you whether she ate more cake! At least this time, she received some outfits that actually fit her! Thank you, family!

Monday was her first doctor's appointment (nine days since our return). I knew our family doctor was anxious to meet our newly adopted daughter. He advised giving her all new immunizations because he wasn't absolutely confident in the immunizations she'd received in Ukraine. He said the medical records were not all legible and wanted to be extra cautious. *Sure, that makes sense.*

I told him what the orphanage director and the judge had said about Shelby's heart and the possibility of her needing some kind of surgery. He carefully listened to her heart and said he didn't hear anything abnormal. Thank God! He examined her thoroughly, checking her weight and height, eyes, ears, and all the rest. He said he didn't have any immediate concerns but would like to see her back every three months for the next year to monitor her progress.

"Progress?" I asked.

"She is underdeveloped, which is to be expected, having been in an orphanage in Ukraine. She did not have proper nutrition and is currently way below her peers on the growth charts," he explained.

"Is there anything Charlie and I should be worried about?" I asked.

"Not at this time," he continued. "She will eventually gain weight just by eating healthy, but you should not give her salt or sugar for at least the next six months. Her system is not used to it."

"Oh really? No sugar or salt?" I smiled, "Ok then, thanks doctor." *Uhhhhhhh..... Too late! How do we undo what's been done? She LOVES CAKE!!!!*

Shelby still wasn't talking after three months. It was time to take her for her three month checkup. I shared my concern with the doctor. He said, "Don't worry. She's processing everything she hears."

I asked, "But, do you think she might be deaf?"

"No, she's not deaf," he said. "She only heard Russian spoken for the first two years of her life. Now she's hearing a new language and has to process it all. I'm sure she'll start talking soon. Be patient. Just give it some time."

"I sure hope you're right," I responded, "because I talk to her all the time, but she just stares at me." The doctor assured me I had no reason to worry. *Just give it some time,* he says.

Deaf or not, I had to do something. If she only understands Russian and I don't, then maybe I can teach her some sign language. It worked! Soon, she was signing several words: more, please, thank you, mom and dad, eat, drink, milk, water, play, yes, no, etc. I kept telling myself, *'Just give it some time.'*

During those first few months, Shelby exhibited some strange behaviors. She still wanted to hold onto food after a meal. She would keep a small chunk of bread or a cracker or other leftover in her hand and wouldn't let go so we allowed her to take whatever she wanted, hoping she would eventually realize she didn't need to worry about having enough to eat. However, those leftovers would somehow find their way into her bed and other places around the house. I would even find food stuffed inside her clothing inside the dresser drawers!

There was another odd discovery in her bedding and on her clothing. Charlie and I kept finding small pea-sized balls of fuzz everywhere. We were perplexed. What were these tiny fuzzy little balls doing all over Shelby's bed and where were they coming from? I thought maybe a stuffed animal had a hole in it and she was pulling the stuffing out. I searched and searched but couldn't find the culprit. Then, Shelby started having nose bleeds almost every day. What's going on? One morning, as I was holding a cloth to her bloody nose, I noticed some of those fuzz-balls inside her nose! On closer inspection, I found several little balls stuck way up inside her nostrils! Now I was worried! What was she doing? Stuffing bits of cotton fuzz into her own nose? Why?

I called our doctor and described what had been happening. He said Shelby's actions must be a habit she had developed in Ukraine. He thought maybe she'd been so bored in the orphanage that she found a way to entertain herself by pulling cotton off blankets and rolling it into little balls. He didn't know why she would stuff her nose with them but what he said was understandable, given the fact that Charlie and I had observed no toys inside the orphanage and wondered what the kids did all day. I asked the doctor what we should do. He recommended we remove all cotton fabrics and stuffed animals from her room! That was not an easy task, but eventually with all fuzz producing culprits removed, she quit picking and rolling and the nose bleeds stopped.

She still wasn't talking when I took her for her six month check-up. The doctor checked her over and gave her some shots (immunizations). He said she was progressing nicely and didn't find anything to be concerned about. I was very concerned about her not yet talking. The doctor said, "She will talk. She's still processing English. It *will* happen."

A couple of days later, I was in the kitchen about to make some breakfast when Cody came in, plopping himself into a chair at the dining room table. I asked him if Shelby was awake. He replied, "I don't know." I went into her room, finding her awake, standing up in her crib, holding the sides of the railing, smiling. Suddenly, she looked up at me and said, "Mom, I want pancakes!"

She was talking! Perfect English! And she talked and she talked. A few weeks after that, I wished she would *stop* talking! I missed all that quiet time.

# KIEV Ukraine

This is a historical Orthodox cathedral in Kiev. The inside was beautiful and very quiet with lots of antiques and ancient sculptures.

(above) Charlie standing in front of cathedral on Wednesday morning. It was about 40° in Kiev and most of the snow had melted.

(below) A casino right across from the cathedral. Alex told us they keep the gates locked to the casino so the poorer people don't lose all their money because they can't afford to gamble. We exchanged our U.S. dollars for the Ukraine currency "grivna" across from here.

(above) This is our interpreter, Alex, standing next to our car. He was very fluent in English. This is also across from the cathedral we visited in Kiev.

# Kharkiv Ukraine

Kharkiv was the first capital of the Ukrainian Soviet Socialist Republic, from December 1919 to January 1934, after which the capital relocated to Kiev. Kharkiv is roughly 300 miles to the east of Kiev. It took us 9 hours by train.

Historical sites lined the streets in Kharkiv in 1999. Here are some we saw from our car as we drove by.

(right) This is a WWII memorial dedicated to the Red Army Soldiers who fought for Kharkiv from 1943 to 1945.

# Kharkiv Ukraine

(below) Small kiosks (shops) along the streets where people can purchase drinks, food, and various other items.

(above) This is the building where we went to get Shelby's birth certificate. It began to snow again when we arrived.

(right) We met with the judge to finalize the adoption at this temporary courthouse which was being renovated at the time. It was previously an elementary school.

*McDonalds!!*

(left) I believe I could actually reach out the window and touch the car next to us as we drove along the unmarked streets of Kharkiv. We spotted a McDonalds and asked if we could go there, but were told by our driver and interpreter that it cost too much, so we relented.

# Kharkiv Ukraine

(above) To the left you can see one of the trolleys that ran via overhead wire through **Kharkiv**.

(above) **This is the post office we went to for postage and to mail documents. It was very small.**

(right and below) Two different buildings near the military academy.

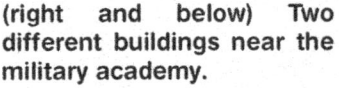

# The Orphanage

(above) Charlie outside the orphanage on November 12. The exterior is tile and brick and the weather that day was damp and dreary. Many orphans are cared for inside these walls.

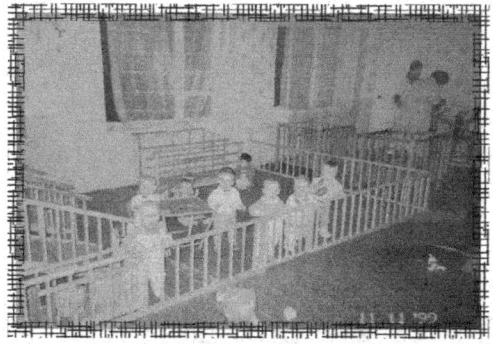

(left) Really no toys to speak of. The children gather at the railing each time we come in; they are curious who we are and what we are doing there.

(right) The little blonde haired boy on the far left in a crib by himself was the "little survivor" we were told about. Always smiling. He had been found inside a trash bag abandoned at birth. We considered adopting him too, but couldn't afford it. I wonder what has happened to him. I hope he has found a "forever home" with a loving family.

# The Orphanage

(left) Meet Shelby Maryna held by her soon to be "forever dad." Isn't she pretty? This is just outside the main children's room at the orphanage during one of our daily visits.

(right) Shelby Maryna loves the cookies we brought to her. She's still warming up to us.

(left) Dinner time! A scoop of soup in a bowl and the kids dig in! Shelby is anxiously waiting for her share (seated here at the top just under the caregiver's pot). Each has a small chunk of bread in thier hand. They all seem to love the camera.

# The Orphanage

November 16..... Adoption Day! Photos taken on our last day at the orphanage. This is the caregiver that Shelby really liked. She was always friendly toward us.

(left) One last goodbye from Charlie and Shelby to all of her little friends. They all wanted to be in the final photos.

(right) November 14th Here we are with our interpreter, Pavlov, and driver, Maxim along with one of the ladies working at the orphanage. That's me holding Shelby.

# Kharkiv Apartment

(below) Tiny apartment in Kharkiv. Looking from the living room into the open entry area. You can see the two doors which open (see below photo) to a toilet and separate tub and sink.

(above) Charlie trying to rest a bit while I take photos of our living space. Two chairs, an end table, and a narrow fold down sofa bed.

(right) Tiny kitchen with small wooden dining table and stools.

# Kharkiv Apartment

Looking out the window from our tiny apartment in Kharkiv at all the towering apartment buildings in our complex. They had no modern cable systems, thus the antenna attached to the exterior of the window.

(left) Nov. 16th, our final day in Kharkiv. We didn't stay overnight in the Kharkiv apartment after we had Shelby with us. We had just enough time to share a final meal with her in the tiny kitchen before heading to the train station for our return to Kiev.

# KIEV Ukraine

Nov. 17th. Back at the original host apartment in Kiev. Happy to have a wonderful spread of various foods to share together. Thank you Emma! You are an amazing cook!

(above) Nov. 20th, our last day in Kiev. Klara brought her daughter Darya to meet Shelby and they had a great time playing together.

(right) One last photo together with our awesome coordinator, Klara. She was a top-notch worker and made us feel comfortable with her unrelenting focus on making our adoption journey successful. Thank you Klara!

# KIEV Ukraine

Nov. 18 Sightseeing in Kiev on a cold and snowy day. We had to keep Shelby covered up.

(below) Our interpreter and driver in Kiev, Alex and Viktor.

(below) Charlie, Shelby and Alex.

# HOME at last

11-24-99 Back home in Broken Arrow, Oklahoma. Above is the welcome home banner Cody created along with some photos of Cody with Shelby, his new little sister.

# Shelby
## senior year

## today

# Confirmations

## June, 1999

Our family attended St. Mark's United Methodist Church in 1999. After service one Sunday, we participated in a potluck fundraiser for our church. The activity building had been set up for a silent auction with lunch. Long tables were placed around the room with auction items placed on them, ready for people to place their bids. I always enjoyed silent auctions and thought it was a great way to have a fundraiser. Men, women and children were already making their way to the auction tables.

Charlie and I sat down to eat with my parents and others, but Cody wanted to go look at the auction items. He couldn't wait. He asked if he could bid on something. We told him, "Yes, but not over $10." Off he went while we ate and visited with family and friends.

Cody returned and quickly ate some food, then jumped up and raced back to the tables. I think he was checking to be sure no one placed a bid higher than his. I asked Cody if he'd bid on anything. He said, "Yes. I put $10 on it. I hope I get it!" Once bidding closed, we were told everyone who won would be notified at church the next Sunday and could pay for their items at that time. I didn't know if Cody's bid had won the item he wanted. I didn't even know what he'd bid on.

The following Sunday, the secretary from our church handed me a small paper bag stapled shut with Cody's name on it. She said Cody had won the item from the auction. I asked her how much we owed. She said, "Well, Cody put $10 on the item, but no one else even put a bid on it. You don't have to pay that much. Anything is fine."

I said, "Oh, no. We'll happily pay $10. It's for a good cause."

I gave her a ten dollar bill and handed the bag to Cody. He didn't open it. He said it was a gift for his new sister when she came to live with us. At that, I didn't ask what it was. *What a sweet gesture.*

When we returned home from our trip to Ukraine with our new little girl, Cody ran to his room and reappeared with that small paper bag in his hands. I watched as he opened it and pulled out a small stuffed animal and handed it to his new little sister. She took it and smiled. I hugged both of them. Shelby reached up, holding the little animal in her hands, to show me. I took it from her and noticed it had a small tag attached at the floppy ear. It was a TY Beanie Baby. I opened the red, heart shaped tag and read the name: SHELBY.

## September, 1999

I'll never forget the day I got so upset with Charlie while he was working on the room remodel at our house and we were arguing about whether to build shelves in the corner of the room. Every day/hour brought more tension to our lives awaiting an answer. I had gone to my bathroom and called out to God for an answer. I practically demanded He give me a sign that day! And He did! The acceptance letter from Ukraine arrived in the mail that day.

You may think it's just a coincidence, the letter was already in the mail, so we would have received it no matter what. I might agree with that theory had I not found out the following Monday, from Dillon, that they themselves had been late mailing our dossier to Washington and Ukraine hadn't received it until late August. Dillon was shocked to hear we'd received the acceptance letter so soon. They said they'd never seen approval happen that quickly. All previous applications had been taking nearly six months. Ours happened in three weeks! God did it! There's no other way to explain it.

## November, 1999

During one of the phone calls back home while we were in Kharkiv, I asked my mom to call our family doctor and make an appointment for us to take Shelby for a physical upon our return. I had given my mom the name, 'Shelby,' along with her birth date. That's all I told her. My mom had called our doctor the next day to make an appointment for us to bring our newly adopted daughter for her first visit. The receptionist asked for more information about Shelby. My mom told her she didn't have anything else to share. The doctor's office needed to put down a first, middle and last name. Mom didn't know the middle name, but told them to put down a middle initial, M. She didn't know what Shelby's birth name was or that Charlie and I had decided to use her birth name as her middle name, Maryna.

Later, I asked mom how she knew her middle name started with "M." She said, "I didn't. I just blurted out, 'Put down M.'"

## November, 1999

While in the process of visiting Shelby at the orphanage, we met other couples who were adopting children. They were from various states in the U.S. One particular couple shared their experience with us. The man told us they had been in Ukraine for nearly a month and still didn't have a court date. He said they'd had nothing but problems. They couldn't believe our process was moving so quickly.

Another young couple told us they had actually done their adoption on their own. They hadn't used an adoption agency or attorney. That surprised me! They said they had been there nearly two months! They wanted to know how we were able to do this so fast. Of course, I said, "Our adoption agency is wonderful and God was in this from Day One!"

At the time, Charlie and I hadn't thought much about how the process was unfolding. We just accepted it, but after hearing from others about how their adoptions were going, we understood how fortunate we were. We attributed a lot to the great work of Dillon International and ultimately to God.

In thinking back at this point, it's interesting that we actually began the process on March 5th and returned from Ukraine with a little girl on November 23rd. Nine months—the length of a pregnancy.

## March to November, 1999

Leading up to the trip, I had been praying for several months, asking God to let Shelby know we would be coming to get her. I wanted Him to let her know so she could, in turn, let us know who she was when we arrived. I know that sounds strange, but I like to be very specific with my prayers. I always have been. So when we met Shelby for the first time at the orphanage, sitting in the small director's office, what did she do? She reached out to Charlie. The director then told us that she had been labeled, "Unadoptable" because she refused to accept men. She said she'd been at the orphanage a year and they had tried to 'get her adopted' several times, but she would scream out whenever a man tried to hold her. The director said Shelby (Maryna) had never allowed a man to hold her. Was her reaching out to Charlie her way of "letting us know?" *It's me. Here I am. I've been waiting for you. God told me you were coming!*" Remember, the first little girl they brought in was crying so much the caregiver had to remove her. Then the second little girl (Shelby) was brought in and had never allowed a man to hold her. Until Charlie.

## June, 2009

Several months after I'd heard from God ("I want you to tell your story"), I found myself struggling with the whole idea of actually writing a book, even doubting whether God had actually told me to. I questioned Him again, *Is this really what you want? I'm not a writer, Lord! I can't do it."*

Weeks would go by while I questioned whether God had truly told me to write a book. Then one day in June, I went to my hairdresser for a cut and color. I'd been there several times over the last couple years and the lady who cut my hair was a Christian. While she worked on my hair, we talked about God, faith, and family. I told her how God had told me to write a book about my adoption experience. She thought it was wonderful! She even told me she knew a Christian publisher that could help me when I was ready. *Oh no! I'm not ready!* I had not even started and was actually procrastinating, trying to find excuses NOT to write this book!

God wasn't leaving me alone on this. He placed support people in my life, each one encouraging me to do what God wanted. Even my Sunday school teacher said, "Write your heart out!" Wow, they're all telling me to write the book, but how?

When I left the salon and got in my car, I prayed, "God, if you really want me to write this book, then please give me another confirmation." Yes, like Gideon, putting out the fleece again. I had to know for sure. It was a Wednesday, and I knew we'd be at church that night. I asked God to have someone, anyone, mention the adoption before the end of the day. I would accept that sign as confirmation. I went home and didn't think about it again.

Around 5 p.m., while sitting at my sewing machine, I heard Charlie come in. He was home earlier than I'd expected. I looked up as he approached and said, "Hi there. You're home early."

He replied, "Yeah, had a few detours today. You'll never guess who called me this afternoon."

I said, "Oh. Who?"

He asked, "Do you remember the pastor of that church over in east Tulsa. The church I did some remodeling in that used to be a barn?"

I thought a minute and replied, "Yes, I think I remember. Several years back, right? You built some walls inside?"

He continued, "Yes. Anyway, he called me out of the blue and said he'd thought of me when he'd received a phone call from a couple in his church who were interested in foreign adoption."

I immediately turned from my sewing and looked up at Charlie.

"Really?" I said.

"Yeah, he wanted to know if it would be alright for the couple to contact us about our adoption. I told him, yes, that would be fine. Weird, huh?" Charlie said.

I was dumbfounded. I couldn't speak. I cried and laughed and Charlie asked if I was ok. I proceeded to tell him about my prayer that afternoon regarding God telling me to write this book.

God didn't wait for me to go to church to have someone bring up the adoption. He answered my prayer with the first person I encountered after leaving the salon. Amazing!

# Conclusion

It's been over twenty years since the night Cody asked, 'Why can't we go get one of those kids?' A lot happened in those twenty years. Charlie and I faced many hurdles while raising little Shelby Maryna. I could literally write another book about everything that transpired, but then again, unless God tells me to, don't expect one.

Since the adoption, I have asked God many times, "Why? Why me? Why our family? Why such a huge, life changing assignment? Why did you bring Shelby into our lives? Do you have a special plan for her?" I've never received a direct answer, nor should I expect to. God owes me nothing. He asked me to do something and I did. I believe He used me to bring glory to Him, both by giving a child a better life and by sharing this story with you. I believe He wanted me to grow in my faith. He taught me how to be more humble, how to respond to Him and trust Him. I believe God can use anyone who is willing to listen and step out into the unknown.

Shelby was not in need of any medical attention. Her heart turned out to be perfectly healthy. She only suffered from malnutrition that was quickly resolved by feeding her American food, which she devoured!

Charlie lost 15 pounds while we were in Ukraine! Me? None. Nyet. Zip. Zero.

The room remodel did get done and I helped paint the walls, lay the floor tile, and hang curtains. It looked very nice. Charlie knew what he was doing. Of course, I knew that all along. We were able to use the room as our home office, allowing Shelby to have her own bedroom.

Cody graduated from high school in 2009 and went to college at the University of Oklahoma, then moved to Michigan to get his master's degree from Michigan State University. He did it all in less than five years! He decided to stay in Michigan (much to my dismay) and now has a great job up there plus a wonderful young lady in his life. They are planning a wedding next year! Can't wait! Grandkids soon?

My older two children, from my first marriage, have both achieved success in their careers. My oldest daughter achieved her Ph.D. and now teaches at an Arts college in New England. She's married but has no children of her own. My oldest son lives in Tulsa, has a great job and is still single.

Not long after Shelby came to us, I gave up my 25 year career as a graphic artist and manager to become a stay-at-home-mom; it was something that I had never been able to do while raising my other children. I went back to college part time to become a sign language interpreter which allowed me to work in the education system on my own schedule. I was able to later homeschool Shelby and interpret in the schools part time.

Little Shelby Maryna is all grown up. She's gifted at writing and music, and she loves children and traveling. Currently, she's living in Ohio so we try to talk on the phone at least once a week and text often. And, of course, there's Facebook and Facetime! She told me recently that she made a new friend, another young lady from Ukraine! I pray for Shelby every day.

As parents, we all want the best for our kids. We want to see them reach adulthood, go out into the world and make a difference, right? Charlie and I did the best we could to raise our children to be humble, honest, hard-working, and grateful for what God has given them. We taught them to give their best and to treat others as themselves. Hopefully, with God's help, they will make a difference in this world and have children of their own one day.

In February, 2009, my dad died. He had suffered from Type II diabetes and been on weekly dialysis for several years that led to the loss of one leg. It was difficult to watch my hero in physical decline. Losing my dad was very hard on me. No longer could I just pick up the phone and ask his opinion on things. I would have loved his advice and input on this book. I wish he could have seen Cody graduate from high school just three months later. I wish he could have seen Shelby grow up. He would have been proud of them. I miss him so much.

My mother celebrated her ninetieth birthday recently! She is in great health and still drives to church, walks her dog, plays cards, works jigsaw puzzles, and enjoys living in her own home.

She is a proud representative of the "greatest generation" and I believe she is one of the greatest of all.

In early December, 2015, Shelby turned eighteen and a few days later she moved out of our home. Charlie and I didn't want her to leave, in fact, we tried everything to get her to stay, but she had made up her mind. We had to let her go. I never fully understood why the urgency to be on her own. Perhaps it was her independent nature (can't imagine where she got that from). Suddenly we found ourselves "empty nesters." With all the kids grown and gone, Charlie and I were able to say we had completed the "raising children" chapter and were looking forward to the next chapter in our lives. What does God have in store for us?

A week after Shelby left, on Saturday, December 12th, Cody arrived from Michigan to spend a couple weeks with us during the holidays. We hadn't seen him since May and were excited to have him home. Three days after Cody arrived, on the morning of December 15th, Charlie left early to go to a job site. He, along with another worker, were doing some repairs to the side of a building while sitting on top of separate ladders. Suddenly, the ladder Charlie was on gave way. He fell, hitting his head on concrete. One of the business owners called me around 10 a.m., saying Charlie was being taken to the hospital by ambulance.

I didn't know the full extent of his injuries when I received the call but really wasn't too concerned because Charlie was always getting injured and had been to the E.R. many times in the past. Each time, he was stitched up and returned to work the next day! However, this time was different. His heart had stopped, yet somehow the paramedics were able to secure a heartbeat while transporting him to the hospital. Cody and I rushed to the emergency room, not yet fully knowing what had happened. Upon arrival, we were led to a private room where we were informed of the seriousness of Charlie's injuries. He'd broken both wrists and had sustained multiple skull fractures.

The prognosis was grim. It didn't look good, they said. What does that mean? Everything they were telling me began to slowly sink in, but it still didn't seem real. Surely it wasn't as bad as they were saying, was it? I mean, this can't be happening, can it? We were just about to begin our next chapter! He has so much more to do! *We* have more we want to do together!

They had placed him on life support. Several brain scans were administered over the next three days, each one confirming our worst fears. Church members, family, and friends all prayed for a miracle, but none came. Charlie never regained consciousness or brain activity. On Friday, December 18th, Cody and I made the heart wrenching decision to remove life support. Charlie took his last breath Sunday morning at about the same time we would have been preparing to go to church. He was 63 years old.

In an instant, life changes. A child is born, a natural disaster strikes, a loved one is diagnosed with a terminal illness, and a family member dies. Life happens. Death happens. Change happens. None of us know what tomorrow may bring or even if we will breathe our next breath. We only know God is in control of those tomorrows—those breaths.

After Charlie died, I was scared. I felt alone but I knew I wasn't alone. God reassured me that He would provide. I only have to call out to Him. He has always taken care of me and after the loss of my husband, God was there. Cody and Shelby were there. My mom and sisters were there. And my church family was there as well. I'm so grateful for all their love and support.

I decided after Charlie's death, with Cody and Shelby now on their own, to sell the house we'd shared in Broken Arrow for close to twenty five years and move in with my mom and my younger sister, who had lost her husband as well. God willing, my sister and I will take care of our mom during the remaining years of her life.

I have returned to work full-time as a deaf education interpreter in the public schools. I love working with the elementary age children. This is where God has planted me so I'll continue to trust Him to use me however He chooses.

Recently, during a Wednesday night bible study at my church, my pastor, Guy Harrell, said, "God doesn't involve Himself in the affairs of men. He involves men in the affairs of God." When he said that, I was reminded again how God did exactly that when He called on me to adopt a child from a foreign country. He wasn't inserting Himself in *my* plan. He made the plan and placed me in it. Just like He used Moses, Jonah, and Gideon; He used me to accomplish His goal. My response is simply to give Him glory and honor.

When God first told me to write this book, I panicked! I didn't know how to begin. But then I remembered all those hand-written notes I had made on the backs of old pay stubs while we were in Ukraine. I still had them. I had actually kept them inside a photo album I'd created from our trip. Wow! It was for this reason God impressed on me to write down each day what transpired during the adoption journey! He knew then that He would call on me later to tell my story!

I did not feel confident at all. I'm not a writer. I love to read books but never thought I'd be writing one! Again, it wasn't my idea. I kept telling myself I couldn't do it. I even enrolled in some college courses on writing. Even that didn't help build any confidence. I was just scared to try—afraid I would fail. Once again, I needed more faith. Then God reminded me, when He calls, He equips. (Read Exodus 4:10-11.) Eventually, I accepted the challenge. "Ok, Lord. I'll do it. I'll trust you to provide the words and the way."

I began by copying all my handwritten notes from those pay stubs and while copying, I recalled more and more from our trip. I wrote more notes. Then, I started wondering how to begin the book; where should I start? I thought about where the journey had begun. The beginning—20/20. I started there and more memories flooded back. Looking at the pictures I'd taken helped fill in gaps. After that, I trusted God for the rest.

I would be remiss if I didn't share how visiting the country and people of Ukraine also changed my life. We spent time with two different families who had very little. Each day, I watched as the wife would leave early in the morning with an empty bag and return a short time later with the same bag filled with just enough food to last one day. There were no food pantries. They did not spend money on frivolous things or have any items of value in their tiny apartments. They had only what they needed to survive from one day to the next. I was dropped into their culture and realized how different it was from mine. I cried every day while we were in Ukraine and acquired a new appreciation for humanity itself.

We learned from Klara that the caregivers working in the orphanage were paid next to nothing in wages by the state. The monthly income for these workers equated to $19! Nineteen dollars a month! Pondering this fact, I began to understand why many people who live in, not just Ukraine, but other third world countries, believe that all Americans are rich and wasteful. The people we stayed with in Ukraine were grateful for the opportunity to host us and earn some extra money. They treated us with respect every step of the way. My heart aches for these people and their country.

Although we were only there a short while, I feel blessed to have had the opportunity to meet some of the people of Ukraine. They were warm and welcoming to us. I'm grateful to have known them and still think about each of them to this day. Never was I more thankful to be an American than while I was in Ukraine. I think every American should visit a place like this. We are so blessed to live in a country where we have plenty. Most of us will never know how others live around the world. We should not take for granted what God has given us. I never will.

God has a plan. He uses people who are willing to answer His call. He used me (an unworthy, fallible human) to accomplish His will. He planted a seed. I tested the soil and eventually allowed the seed to grow. I doubted. I pushed back. I was weak and afraid. It's all about faith. I had to let go of my own selfish desires and allow God to take over. I had to trust and believe completely in order to let God lead me.

I am far from perfect and have failed over and over in my life, but I'm still trying each and every day to answer the call and watch for seeds. When I see them, I ask these questions: Do they reinforce all the things Jesus taught? Are they grounded in the written word of God? Do they ultimately bring glory to God? I will keep listening, praying, reading, working, serving, and most of all, remain ready to do His will. Yes, whatever it may be! *And I'll always give you, Lord, all the credit.*

• • •

*Thank you, Lord, for trusting me. Thank you for Shelby. I don't understand all your ways, but I believe I can ask you anything and I know that all things are possible with you. If it be your will, Lord, I ask you to give peace to Shelby's birth mother, wherever she may be. Please let her know that her baby was given a good life. Amen.*

• • •

I asked Shelby if she would like to contribute anything to my book. Here's what she wrote.

## December, 2020

> "We might not share DNA,
> but we do share soul."
> —Lauren Meely

My parents' efforts to connect with my culture as a family was extremely raw and beautiful. One of the first things I remember was attending a Russian language class as a family. My dad, mom, brother, and I would go together on Tuesdays and always go out afterward to eat at the same restaurant every week.

Another thing I remember is my mom having treasures that she acquired while she was in the Ukraine. She would keep them on a high shelf and I always knew they were special. She would let me have chocolate she got from there, take my Matryoshka dolls to show and tell, and play with my Russian alphabet blocks.

I was adopted when I was two. I didn't realize how lucky I was to be adopted and growing up in America until I was a teen. During my childhood, my parents made friends with other families who also adopted. Every year, my family would celebrate my "adoption day" by taking me out to eat. In middle school, I met other students who were also adopted. It made me feel connected. When I was 17, I finally became a U.S. citizen, which was super exciting!

Now that I'm in my 20s, I enjoy reading about Ukrainian culture, trying Russian food at the market, and holding those traditions dear to my heart from when I was younger. All these things that my parents did to instill my culture in me when I was a child make me still appreciate it to this day.

It warms my heart how supportive my extended family was of my parents' decision to adopt. I am also so thankful for my brother for mentioning the idea of adoption, and being so welcoming all these years. Above all, I am forever grateful to my parents who traveled all the way across the world to adopt me.

Shelby

• • •

*Faith is taking the first step,*
*even when you don't see the whole staircase.*
*—Martin Luther King, Jr.*

*Ye have not chosen me, but I have chosen you,*
*and ordained you, that ye should go and bring forth fruit,*
*and that your fruit should remain: that whatsoever ye shall*
*ask of the Father in my name, he may give it you.*
*John 15:16 (KJV)*

*For with God nothing shall be impossible.*
*Luke 1:37 (KJV)*

*Trust in the Lord with all thine heart; and lean not*
*unto thine own understanding. In all thy ways*
*acknowledge him, and he shall direct thy paths.*
*Proverbs 3: 5-6 (KJV)*